My Master

Shri Ram Chandraji
Founder-President
Shri Ram Chandra Mission

My Master

by
Shri Parthasarathi Rajagopalachari

Shri Ram Chandra Mission
USA

First Edition	January 1975:	1500 Copies
Second Edition	August 1976:	1000 Copies
Third Edition	July 1979:	1500 Copies
Fourth Edition	May 1985:	2000 Copies
Fifth Edition	August 1989:	2000 Copies

© Shri Ram Chandra Mission
North American Publishing Committee
Pacific Grove, CA, USA, 1989

ISBN 0-945242-12-3

Contents

Foreword

In the postscript to the previous editions of this book, I have related an experience which led to the writing of this book in 1974. It was the result of what I believe to have been an inner command from my Master, from within me. I shall now try to relate what happened earlier to that, which may explain why the command of the Master was issued to me.

My Master had been seriously ill in the early part of the year 1974, and had to be finally hospitalised in Lucknow, where he lay in deep coma for almost one month. In view of his advanced age — he being 75 years old then — there were deep, though unexpressed, fears that the end may not be long. It was very much of a miracle to most of us when he regained consciousness, and then went on to regain his health.

It was my privilege to have been with him for part of the time he was hospitalised. I also went to Shahjahanpur after he was discharged from the hospital in Lucknow, and stayed with him for many days till he was relatively in better health, after his month long ordeal. It was then that he revealed to me that he had chosen me to be his spiritual representative, to eventually succeed him as the President of the Mission, whenever that became necessary. Those were, for me, very moving days, driving me to tears from moment to moment. Those were the blessed days when his gentle and deeply abiding love flowed upon me, over me, like a spring drizzle under blazing sunshine. Those were also the days of the most personal intimacy between us, when there seemed to be nothing at all between us, excepting our two identities. It was as if he had removed all barriers between ourselves, and we were blissfully together in a oneness that would perhaps be difficult to experience later.

It was a time of the greatest happiness for me, and, rather surprisingly, the time of the greatest sorrow for me too, for it was then that I had to face the certain knowledge that one day my beloved would leave me to go into the brighter world. This knowledge almost broke my heart. He could of course divine it at a glance, and he would gently chide me for such thoughts, saying, "I shall be with you for many more years. Do not worry about it now. Mrs. Davies had told me that I shall live till 2006 or 2007, and others have also told me the same thing. So don't cry now. I shall be with you for a long time. One day we all shall have to go. But I repeat, it is very far off." Thus he would chide me and comfort me. But nevertheless, I could not bear to think of the time when he would not be with me, and thus began for me the hidden sorrow in my heart, which has never left me, and which, in 1983, became the stark and devastating reality that shall haunt me for the rest of my life.

This knowledge made me brood over what I should do to try to show my love for Him, and to express my gratitude to Him, for the gifts of His love that I have received were no small gifts! This made me brood all the time about what I should do, with the result that an inner pressure was steadily built up in my heart, and the need became obsessive. It was in this frame of mind and heart that I was in Madurai — and there the miracle occurred, of His inner instruction to me, resulting in the writing of this book.

It is my conviction that such an inner pressure has to be built up, by our own effort, and then His help crystallises within us, and then all becomes possible. Love for Him alone can make this possible.

8th March 1989
Bangalore   P. Rajagopalachari

Part I

The Master

"*I am a Lamp to thee who beholdest Me,*
I am a Mirror to thee who perceivest Me,
I am a Door to thee who knockest at Me,
I am a Way to thee a wayfarer."

(Hymn of Jesus, from The Apocalyptic Acts of John)

I

The First Exposure

I was drawn into the Mission at the end of March 1964 by Shri Vira Raghavan, preceptor-in-charge of the Madras centre. Before I joined this great organisation I had not even heard its name! Shri Vira Raghavan and my father had become friends through a common interest in homoeopathy. Shri Vira Raghavan used to visit us occasionally, generally to have a medical look at my son and to offer advice for treatment on those occasions when he fell sick. My contact with him then was quite tenuous, being restricted to polite exchanges of greetings. One day in February (a very fortunate one for me!) Shri Vira Raghavan happened to see some of the books I was interested in − yoga, psychology, philosophy, mysticism, etc. He said, "Since you are interested in this sort of thing, why don't you try a practical approach?" I answered that I had done a few things for quite some years but, lacking guidance, I had given up practical pursuit of yogic sadhana. Then Shri Vira Raghavan said, "A few of us sit together and meditate. If you are interested you can join us and try out our method." I accepted instantly. My father joined the 'sitting' the very next Sunday, which happened to be Vasant Panchami day. My induction was however delayed by several weeks since I had to leave Madras on official work.

At that time Shri Vira Raghavan did not make any specific mention of Master, or tell us of the importance of the Master in this system of yoga. All that we saw was a photograph at which I, for one, glanced just casually. There was no particular impact other than a mental idea, "Oh! This is the person who guides the students. Very good!" Shri Vira Raghavan told us that this gentleman from Shahjahanpur had come the previous year, but we were not then made aware of his visit. Shri Vira Raghavan told us that we had been informed, albeit casually, of his visit the previous year. I then recollected Shri Vira Raghavan telling us the previous year that his *acharya* had come to Madras, and he would therefore be busy for a few days until his *acharya* left. At that time we had taken him to mean that his *Vaishnav acharya* had come to pay a visit. Regrettably, Shri Vira Raghavan had not enlightened us fully then, so that one precious opportunity of meeting the Master face to face had been irretrievably lost. Nevertheless, at the time we joined the Mission, this loss was not really felt since we had as yet no idea of the Master. This sense of loss was to come later.

During the middle of 1964 I had to go to Bareilly on official work, and thence to Lucknow. I actually passed through Shahjahanpur but I did not have the address of the Mission Headquarters with me, nor did I bother to try and locate the Mission to have Master's darshan. Thus a second opportunity was lost, this time by my own lack of interest. Within a few months the first sign of Master's grace came in the shape of another call to go to Bareilly, again on company work. After completing my work at Bareilly I proceeded to Shahjahanpur on a Saturday afternoon, leaving my colleagues behind at Bareilly, promising to be back the same evening. I arrived at Shahjahanpur at about 3 p.m., halted arbitrarily at an intersection, and asked for directions on how to get to Master's place. I was directed by the traffic con-

Babuji's Home in Shahjahanpur

stable to a sweet-meat seller a hundred yards away. The sweet-meat stall owner gave me further directions and I found myself at Master's residence, the 'ashram' as it is generally called, just a few minutes later! It had all been so direct and so simple.

I entered the ashram and requested an interview with the Master. I was told that he was resting, but that I could go into his room and sit down there, taking care not to disturb his rest. I found Master on a low bed, lying facing the wall with his back to me. This was my first view of the Master. He was lying on his right side with his knees drawn up, and looked very small and unimpressive as a human person. My first feeling was one of disappointment. "What?", I thought, "Is this the man who is going to lead me to my goal? It looks as if he himself could do with some help in even moving around physically. How then is he going to help me?" For the next half hour my thought followed this strain. It is no secret to say that I was quite disappointed and wished I had not come so far, alone, to see him. As my thoughts came to this dismal conclusion he suddenly turned round, fully awake, and I saw his face. He stared at me, seeming to look right through me, and I stared back at him, rather impolitely I am afraid. I introduced myself as an abhyasi of the Madras centre. He then sat up, back and head bent slightly forward, his body resting on his two hands which held the edge of the cot. He seemed to be ruminating over some inner thought. He appeared to be absorbed, and his face had a rather sombre expression on it. After a few moments he looked up at me again, and I saw his eyes. They are the deepest eyes I have ever seen. Generally human eyes seem to have a backdrop, a limit to transparency. Some eyes are even totally opaque, and one sees nothing but the outer surface of the cornea. In Master, the eyes are completely transparent, and seem to point the way to another world lying behind them. When one looks into Master's eyes, it is as if one is looking up into a clear, blue sky. The gaze goes on and on, limitlessly and for ever, without an end to penetration. Master's eyes seem to contain all space and all creation within them. That look won me over. I could now well believe the puranic stories of Yashoda seeing the whole world in Shri Krishna's baby mouth! I knew immediately and intuitively that I had found the person who alone could be my Master, and lead me to my goal.

Master slowly stood up and went out of the room on to the verandah, and looked around as if searching for something. He then asked me where my luggage was. I told him that I had left my bag in the car on the main road. Without even asking me about my plans he sent someone to bring the car around, to unload my suitcase, and to put it in the room next to the one he had been occupying, all of was which done, thus making my plans for me! He then asked someone else to get me a cup of tea together with something to eat. After this he went into his inner apartments, the family quarters as I found out subsequently, brought a towel, and laid it on the platform near the well which was, in those days, the only source of water. The well had a hand-pump by which water was pumped out. He put a bucket under the spout and pumped it full of water. After this he came and sat in his chair, smiled, for the first time, and said, "Please have your bath, the water is ready." My first reaction was one of chagrin that I had permitted an old man, far above my years, to draw my bath for me. The next one was of something I can hardly give expression to, even today. It was a conglomerate of emotions, of gratitude, awe, and love all mixed up together, along with a lot of shame in it. Shame because I had stood by and watched him pumping away to fill the bucket, imagining he was filling it up for himself, and had not offered to help him at all! All along I had wanted to go and do the pumping, but my shyness had prevented this. Anyway I had my bath as instructed, just by the well in the open, as the ashram had no bathroom in those days. By then the tea had arrived and I refreshed myself. After this I just sat on the verandah, while the Master kept at his own routine, frequently getting up to go inside the house to give instructions to the household staff and so on. Master also introduced me to the first person I had met when I entered the ashram, Shri Ishwar Sahai, whom I discovered to be Master's personal assistant and permanent companion.

Master had assumed I would stay the night, and I did not tell him I had to go back the same evening. I did not inform him of my plan, lacking the courage to do so. So I just sat and sat, waiting for something to happen. At about 7 o'clock Master went inside the house, and almost immediately came out to ask me whether I ate onions. I answered that I did not. I was puzzled by this question, but assumed that it had some relationship to spiritual practice. He then went in again, stayed away for some fifteen minutes, and then returned to his easy chair on the verandah. At about 8 o'clock someone came and whispered something to him. He immediately got up and said, "Come, your dinner is ready. Please eat it. I have arranged to have some curd brought for you, knowing that South Indians are accustomed to have it at all their meals." I had not expected this but meekly followed him and ate my meal. After finishing dinner I asked permission to leave. Master appeared surprised.

He said, "You have just arrived, and you have come from such a long distance. Can you not stay at least another day?" The invitation to stay was so genuine and affectionate that I could do nothing but respond to it. A few other persons had assembled by this time, all local disciples of Master. We sat around him in a loose circle, but were mostly silent. Occasionally Master made some remark and lapsed into silence again. The evening wore on in this desultory fashion until finally, around 10 o'clock, feeling quite sleepy, I went to bed.

It was, as I found out by later experience of the Master's daily routine, a rather unusual day. Master is generally a charming and vivacious conversationalist, capable of immense humour and wit. He often lapses into periods of taciturnity, but these are few and of short duration. On such occasions he is totally withdrawn, and appears to be far away in another world. But when he speaks he has the gift of presenting his profound philosophical thought in the form of easy dialogue which even a totally unlettered person can understand and assimilate into his being, and apply in his work-a-day life. But all this was yet to come my way in my own personal experience. This first day with Master was to me still something of a disappointment because he had hardly addressed a dozen words to me — and those too of practically no spiritual significance whatsoever. All that he had exposed to me of himself was his gracious courtesy and hospitality as a householder. But one important feature or characteristic I did notice was that in Master this appeared entirely natural, and was patently sincere and fundamental to his nature. There was no ostentation, no sense of unnaturalness, no feeling of being patronised. On the contrary there was a spontaneity in his behaviour as a host that made it as natural as it is for the sun to shine, or for water to wet. For the first time in my life I felt myself to be in the presence of the perfect householder who could be a host to his guest without appearing to be one; who could serve his visitor with humility but without any taint of servility; and who could be a Master to the disciple without the vainglorious and arrogant pomp and bluster that, in India at least, seem to be almost essential prerequisites for the assumption of such elevated positions, particularly in the religious hierarchies. I have been exposed to the presence of many many persons who were reputed to be great souls, sannyasis, saints and so on. My professional career has involved a great deal of travel all over India, and on those official journeys I have had opportunities galore for such encounters. But rarely have I met a 'guru' of even the lowest situation in his own hierarchy where the gurudom had not been tainted by arrogance of manner, ostentation in personal presentation, glibness in making a multitude of promises, and avarice in collecting the disciples' 'gift'. Here, in Shahjahanpur, I had for the first time come across a guru who was simple, direct, unostentatious and unassuming; who made no demands of any kind and yet offered not only the supreme spiritual service of liberation but personal physical service to the abhyasi too. This was, to me, an enigma of shattering proportions and entirely out of tune with the guru of the common run in the Indian environment. So it is not to be wondered at that I went to bed with a welter of confused impressions and thoughts.

I didn't sleep very well that night. There was a large painting of the Grand Master, Lalaji Saheb, on the wall next to my bed, and I had the peculiar impression that he was staring down at me. This made me quite nervous and restless. I kept tossing and turning, and, even in the dark, I continued to feel Lalaji's penetrating eyes boring into me, penetrating through to my very soul, as it were. I woke up early in the morning and was ready by 6 a.m. I found no one about as yet. By the side of Master's easy chair on the verandah a hookah had been prepared ready for him. I learnt that Babuji, as the Master is affectionately called, began his day with the hookah. True enough he appeared at 7 a.m., went straight to his chair, and began pulling away at the hookah. It took some time for the hookah to 'smoke' properly. All this time he was sitting relaxed, completely silent, with a far away look in his eyes. He had a glass of milk half way through. When the hookah was smoked out he went into the office room, opened his medicine kit, and took out a bottle of oil which he proceeded to apply to his scalp, rubbing the oil in with vigorous hand movements. He then went for his bath, returning a short while later dressed in his usual fashion in a dhoti with a hand-stitched cloth banian covering his upper body. When he wants to be formal he wears a kurta. On public occasions he wears a long coat, coming down to his knees, buttoned up all the way to his neck, and sports a white cap. Occasionally he wears pyjamas too. This represents the complete range of his attire.

Master is very fair in complexion and, though short and spare, is extraordinarily handsome with his beautiful beard. His hands are very expressive, and he uses them often in making frequent gestures during conversation. His feet are very soft and the soles particularly so, being as soft as the petals of a flower. Touching them, one can well understand how the term 'lotus feet' came into existence. Master's feet are really lotus feet in their softness and healthy pink colour. Master speaks fluently in Hindi, Urdu and English. His English is direct and exact. I have never known Master use an ambiguous word or phrase, either in conversation or in correspondence. He is one of that very rare breed of persons who say what they mean, and mean precisely what they say. When questioned he gives immediate and considered answers in a most benevolent manner, making the questioner happy that he has asked a question. I noticed that while Master welcomed questions, he preferred them to be such as concern an individual personally. Master generally dislikes purely theoretical questions seeking merely knowledge rather than advice.

Master is a great artist in the matter of avoiding controversy. I found in him a genuine humility when he disclaimed all knowledge of other systems of thought, philosophy etc., but simultaneously, he was as firm as a mountain where knowledge arising out of his own experience of yoga was concerned. Here he was the Master in every sense of the term, prepared to prove his contention or point by practical demonstration rather than by verbose discussion. I had a demonstration of this trait in him when someone asked about a particular spiritual state. Master smiled and answered, "I cannot explain it to you but, if your samskaras will permit it, I can give you the experience of that condition." In making this slight reservation Master was not hedging. This was but one more example of his deep-rooted humility. He rarely claims outright to be able to do anything. One of his stock statements is, "By my Master's Grace all things can be done. After all he is the doer. If Lalaji wishes, this thing can be done in a moment." Even on this first visit I found in Master this deep, personal, spiritual attachment to his own Master Lalaji, and a sense of total dependence on him seemed to be there.

At first this was slightly confusing to me. "After all," I thought, "he is a Master. Why then does he seem so dependent on Lalaji? Does it indicate a personal sense of weakness? Or does he merely use Lalaji as an excuse to cover up his own deficiencies?" But I found my thoughts were wrong. In no word or act did Master reveal even the slightest sense of doubt or incapacity to handle his own affairs, whether involving discussion or what he called his 'work.' I found he had an enormous and total faith in Lalaji, and this gave him total confidence and an iron will in carrying out his own work. Even on this first day Babuji remarked more than once, "For success in work an unfailing will is necessary. If there is no faith in the Master then the work cannot be done. Doubt is the enemy of spirituality. Doubt really shows lack of faith in the Master."

Around 9 o'clock Master called all of us, about six individuals, inside and gave us a group sitting. The sitting lasted for about 30 minutes. After this he went back to his hookah and later was busy with some correspondence in which he was assisted by Shri Ishwar Sahai. I was shy and nervous of going into the room and sitting with them, though all the others present, obviously members of the Mission for several years, went in. So I remained alone on the verandah till lunch. I ate my lunch at 1 o'clock and requested permission of Master to return to Bareilly. He permitted me to leave. When leaving I suddenly felt a nameless sorrow gripping my heart, a feeling as if I was leaving my own home for a long journey, and something akin to leaving beloved ones behind, and tears sprang into my eyes, a phenomenon I have rarely experienced in my adult life. This lasted for almost half an hour before the sorrow disappeared. There were moments of almost over-powering sorrow before I got back to Bareilly.

I had come to see the Master and had had his dar-shan. All the impressions I had in my mind were chaotic. How to judge this man? How to understand him? How to evaluate his work? And the greatest mystery of it all was, what had he done to create in me that feeling of profound sorrow and distress that welled up in my heart when the moment of parting came? I had known this person for barely 24 hours. How, then, could such a strong emotion come into existence out of such a ridiculously short association — and one so su-perficial and bereft of any sort of intimacy whatsoever? I had arrived as a total stranger and, to my mind, departed a stranger. Or had I? This was the question. True, I may need eons of time to 'know' Master. But did he similarly need a long time to know me and work upon me? No! It could not be so, and the proof was in nothing else but the shattering emotional impact of this first meeting. I felt sure that he had done something in the inner-most recesses of my heart; that a seed had been sown deep down as it were, and that this was the first reaction. So, confused as I was in the superficial level of my existence, deep down a faith was born in me that day that I had found my Master, and that I was treading the right path to my goal. It is Master's divine nature that no one who comes to him goes away disap-pointed, and I for one found an inner fulfilment from this first contact with what I came to label in my mind as 'Divinity'. "Master's work," I thought, "commences with the moment when the first human contact is estab-lished." Later experience indicated I was not entirely correct in this conclusion.

II

The Environment

Master's house is a very old one, parts of it being over a hundred years old, while even the newer additions (excluding the recently built overseas visitors' guest house) are more than a quarter of a century old. It is large and spacious, walled round completely, with a main gate on the western wall and a small door next to it. The gate is generally kept closed, visitors invariably using the small door to its left. Immediately on entering there is a large open courtyard, about a third of which is raised and paved with bricks. As one crosses the courtyard one comes up to the verandah of the main building. This is where Master and his abhyasis spend most of their waking hours. Master has his easy chair facing the gate, while the abhyasis sit facing him, with their backs to the gate.

On my first visit to Shahjahanpur I did not notice anything special about this house. But after two or three visits I discovered that as soon as I walked in through the entrance door, I felt as if I was in a different world altogether. The 'atmosphere' within Master's compound is something unique. It has a spiritual quality which is so subtle that it defies description. On one or two occasions I have actually felt a jerk in my heart as I crossed the threshold to enter the compound. The transition from the outside to the inside of the compound is as sudden and refreshing as a dip in a pool of cold water. The more sensitive the person, the more keenly this is felt. On my first visit to Shahjahanpur I came as a visitor and did not notice any difference. On subsequent visits I found that I came more in the mood, and with the emotion, of one returning to his own home. This emotion became stronger and stronger with repeated visits, until it became so powerful that even as I left Delhi the emotional intensity would commence, and would become more and more deep until it natural-ly and harmoniously melted within just as I entered Master's home. I have often been so shaken by this feel-ing that I have had to rest a little to regain emotional equanimity before going in to meet Master. Nowadays this emotional onslaught often begins even when I am just leaving Madras for Shahjahanpur. A restlessness begins to be felt in the heart, and this restlessness in-creases as the destination comes nearer and nearer, at times assuming the proportions of almost a physical heart-ache. I discussed this with Master. Master laughed and said, "Yes, your observation is correct. Many persons have remarked on it. But I tell you it is all a matter of sensitivity. Develop sensitivity and see what Bliss you can experience. Really speaking, a person must create his own environment wherever he goes! That is the sign of spirituality. When you sit near a real saint of calibre you will feel peace and tranquillity. Many people ask me how to recognise a saint. I tell them that if they experience peace when sitting near him, then there is saintliness in him." I asked Master why this intense restlessness should be there when we come to him. Master said, "It is a good sign. Restless-ness is good. It indicates inner craving for the goal. Really speaking, in an advanced abhyasi the restlessness is always there, but submerged. Now when you think of coming to me the longing begins to develop, and the longing becomes restlessness until the desired goal is reached. So this restlessness comes into the experience. Now you see the environment here. It is unique. It is the experience of almost all abhyasis that there is something unique. It is Lalaji's grace. In such an environment it is possible to grow spiritually in a very short time. You must create such an environment wherever you go. It is quite simple. Then you will find external thoughts do not disturb you; the outside environment does not disturb you. It is like a diver wearing a special suit. He carries his environment with him down into the depths of the ocean, and so the ocean has no fears for him."

Later, after a few years of personal association with Master, I began to visit him at some of the places where he was camping. Here too I found an atmosphere of peace and tranquillity, but the atmosphere changed when he left. When I asked him why this happened, Master laughed and said, "Yes, the change is there as you have seen. But it is not my fault. I create the same atmosphere wherever I go, but what can I do if the people destroy it after I leave? To retain the same atmosphere we must control our thoughts. Thoughts create the atmosphere. If you go to some of the holy places you will find peace there. Why? Because there people come in a spirit of worship and remain calm and prayerful, and so the atmosphere is moulded accordingly. Now if someone should build a cinema or a dance hall in the same place you will find the atmosphere changes immediately, because people now come with other thoughts which modify the atmosphere. So in such places, I mean holy places, we must control our thoughts and guide them in the right direction. Temper and anger must be avoided. Also passion. Because these things can destroy the atmosphere. But even if this happens, the thing can be changed again by meditation and right attitude. I am telling you another thing. It is a very valuable thing. You can 'read' the atmosphere of a place and see what sort of events have taken place there. It is very easy. Just concentrate, and the reading will appear before your eyes. If you go beyond this you can even concentrate on the atmosphere in a general way and 'read' a country's history in it. What happened, when, everything is there. The records of everything are there, clear as anything, but it needs only one who can 'see' to read all this. You would have experienced that sometimes when you enter a new place you feel disturbances. It may be fear, it may be passion. This is automatic and becomes second nature to a sensitive person. Then by Master's grace, if the power is given, you can 'clean' the place. Just imagine Master's grace is flowing through the place and washing away all the impressions. That is all. You see how easy it is! But faith must be there, and a firm will."

I asked Master how to develop sensitivity. Master said, "Develop awareness. Always try to be alert to what is happening, and sensitivity will develop. Many people meditate. But I am sorry to say many of them don't know what is going on in the system during meditation. Why is this? Because they do not watch for what is going on. One has to be alert to the transmission and its action on the system. Then the real joy of meditation begins. Now I tell you one thing. Whether a person has experiences or not, the transmission will work and complete the job. But the real happiness comes when we know what we have got. So sensitivity is necessary. Another benefit is that as you become more sensitive progress becomes faster, because when you know what is being done you can co-operate with the Master actively. So this is a great benefit. But I tell you one thing. Sensitivity is also a curse in another way, because you become 'open' to everything. Everything affects you. I tell you it can cause much suffering and misery. Imagine looking anywhere or at anything or at any person, and immediately the whole thing is before your eyes. How can you remain unaffected? Such a person will be compelled to share in the joys and miseries of all those around him. Sometimes I go to a new place where the atmosphere is so bad that I am almost suffocated. Then I have to clean it, otherwise I could not live in it. So we have to do this cleaning wherever we go. That is why I tell my associates that a Master is really a sweeper, doing a sweeper's job. He attracts all the dirt and uncleanliness, and has to clean them off. That is why they say that for a whole country a single saint of calibre is sufficient. He acts like a big cleaner, cleaning the whole country, because all the grossness is attracted to him. You see this *'tamasha'* (joke), a Master is really a cleaner! That is why I say that a saint is a target for the world's sorrows. So sometimes we have to control sensitivity so that we are not too much affected. Otherwise a sensitive person will become a victim of his environment."

I recall a visit Master once made to a city to visit abhyasis there. I had accompanied him. We were accommodated in the residence of an abhyasi. All went well the whole day, but at night Master was extremely restless, and slept only in fits and starts. When I woke up next morning I found Master quite restless and exhausted. The second night we moved to a nearby hotel, and I was happy that Master slept deeply and continuously right through that night. When he woke up, Master said, "Look here, we are in a hotel where thousands of people come and go, but the atmosphere is better and purer here than at that place. Is it not a shameful thing that the atmosphere in a house should be so gross and dirty while a hotel room is cleaner? What to say of the people who live there in that house. It is a shameful thing that people mould their lives in such a way that their environment is completely polluted and spoilt. Really speaking our minimum duty is to leave the world at least as we found it when we came into it, not spoil it and destroy it. We should really try to leave the world a better place than we found it. Right living becomes very important. We must tune our lives in such a way that everything that comes in contact with us is improved. Everything we touch must get divinised."

I have visited Shahjahanpur very many times and stayed with Master. One thing I have noticed when I am with him is that for the duration of my stay all thought and worry about my home and family evaporate away even as I enter his residence. It is not something that I try to achieve, or pray for. I am not even conscious of it. Yet the effect is that all thoughts of home, family and indeed the whole world outside the ashram seem to leave the mind, to find entry again only when I am finally out of the ashram. This total lack of care, or care-free attitude of mind, is a boon and blessing which one is not aware of when it lasts, but one only feels its absence when this mental state or state of consciousness departs. On one grace-saturated occasion when I had the unique privilege of being with Master for three months continuously, I felt this all the more. A letter from home would suddenly make me conscious of the fact that I indeed had a home and a family somewhere. Momentarily I would be back in that other world, perhaps worrying a little about how things were out there, but as soon as I folded the letter and put it away, I would be back in the 'here and now' of Master's Divine Presence, and the memory of all else, briefly awakened, would fade away, leaving me in peace, enjoying a tranquillity that is entirely out of this world. I have often pondered over this and felt that this is a spiritual condition that will bless us at death. We do not forget, for there is no effort on our part to forget. But a state of mind or consciousness comes into existence as a divine gift which transports us to a different level of existence where everything else ceases to be. In this condition one exists in a blissful state of nearness to the Divine, and this proximity has a healing quality about it, a gift of grace, which makes an unconditioned existence not only possible but a fact in our own being and consciousness.

On a lesser level I would like to record one more personal experience of the effect of Master's environment on me. On one occasion I stayed about four weeks continuously at Shahjahanpur with Master. Several more abhyasi brothers and sisters were present, along with Master's own household. One day I had to go to Bareilly for some urgent shopping. As I entered Bareilly I saw a large advertisement put up, advertising a cinema currently showing in the city. The advertisement showed a well-known cinema actress in a suggestive pose, and the idea of sex came into my mind. It was at that moment that I became conscious of the fact that for the last four weeks there had been no consciousness of sex at all in my mind even though there had been men and women all around me! This was a rarely revealing occasion, displaying vividly the capacity of my Master in moulding the environment and the mind of the aspirant.

I have attended the Vasant Panchami celebration at Shahjahanpur as often as I could. This is the only formal celebration the Mission members celebrate annually. It is the birthday of Lalaji, and the celebration is spread over three days. I have found that the atmosphere in Shahjahanpur is something out of this world during those three days. It is quite different from the normal atmosphere. Master confirmed this. He said, "You will not find this atmosphere when the utsav is over. I tell you, during those three days it is as if a blanket or covering is put over this house. And at the end of the celebration, Lalaji seems to catch one corner of the blanket and whisk it off. It is a divine atmosphere during those three days. It is Lalaji's grace. It is so pure and so highly spiritual, it is like living in another world." The only occasion when I have felt the atmosphere to be even more transcendentally pure and glorious was during the three day celebrations at Madras in February 1973 when abhyasis from all over India, and from many centres abroad, congregated to celebrate Lalaji's Birth Centenary. The celebrations were held in hired premises usually let out to celebrate marriages in. The hall is one of the largest and most beautiful available in Madras. I remarked on the special nature of the atmosphere during those three days. Master confirmed my observation and laughingly added, "By Lalaji's grace this place has been so fully charged that it will last for many years. All those who come here will benefit by merely being present here." Yet, when the celebrations concluded and I went to settle up accounts, the place looked so forlorn and empty that I felt like weeping. The life had gone out of the place, and what remained was a mere shell. That special atmosphere of absolute spiritual purity had evaporated.

We were once assembled in the house of Shri Umesh Saxena, Master's son, at Besant Nagar in Madras. It was an informal gathering consisting of about half-a-dozen local abhyasis and two overseas abhyasis. We were all seated on the floor while Master sat on a sofa. The overseas abhyasis had been asking Master a series of questions on a variety of subjects. Somehow the subject veered round to that of the atmosphere and its influence — what we call, in a rather restricted way, environmental influence. Master explained how the atmosphere can change depending on how people think and how they conduct their lives. Master said that all this information was stored in the form of *richas* which a competent saint could read when necessary. Master went on to explain how such conditions could be re-created if and when necessary, how the conditions could be 'drawn down' as it were. The overseas abhyasis were eager to have a practical demonstration of this. Master smilingly agreed. He said he would re-create the atmospheric condition that existed in very ancient times, when man was just emerging into life as a separate class of life. Master sat up straight. His expression became serious. His eyes seemed to concentrate on a point about six feet in front of him, at about the same height above the floor. He sat thus for about two minutes. Suddenly he moved forward and downward thrice, while making a peculiar noise like hmm...hmm...! He then sat still for a minute. Then the tension relaxed, and he smiled and asked us what we felt. I told him I felt the atmosphere to be very gross, heavy and oppressive, and I felt it to have been saturated with primitive terror. Master said this was the correct reading. The overseas abhyasis were somewhat sorry that Master had only allowed this experience to

last for barely a minute. Master laughed and said, "Do
you think you could have borne it for a longer period?
As Parthasarathi said it was charged with terror and
very gross. If you were surrounded by it longer, then it
would have affected you adversely. So I just gave you a
taste of it. You see from what levels human life has
evolved? But all this is not enough. When the divine atmosphere is created then you will really enjoy it. By
Lalaji's grace you will also experience that when you are
ready for it!"

All yogic teachers have advised their students to set
apart a room specially for their prayers and meditation.
The idea behind this of course is to have a room where
the atmosphere is kept pure, uncontaminated by normal life routines. Master's teaching expands this to the
ultimate dimension of a pure and holy universe, where
the whole universe becomes a prayer room. The older
idea is restrictive. It seeks to enclose purity into a small
place, implying that the rest of the home may be impure. Master says this is not sufficient. We may begin at
one point, our own hearts, but the seed of purity sown
there must be nurtured and made to grow in such a
manner that it radiates beyond the confines of the individual human system, radiates beyond his home and
beyond his small world until, finally, the whole universe
comes within its divine embrace.

III

Tolerance

Master is a living example of his own credo that a human being must fly, like a bird, on two wings, one of spirituality and the other of materiality. This is one of the most fundamental and far-reaching lessons of Sahaj Marg. This teaching simply means that a person must not neglect either his physical and material existence or his spiritual life. It is a revolutionary message that Master is broadcasting to the world, and has come when most needed. Indian yogic teachers have, by and large, tended to disparage the physical life as something nasty and unclean, from which an aspirant should run for dear life. The procedures of training prescribed are so complicated and rigid that it is well nigh impossible for an individual to subjugate and control his physical existence within his own span of life. When, therefore, is he to go on to spiritual progress? The only answer possible would seem to be, "In the next life or lives!"

Master teaches that there is nothing wrong with material creation and with a human's material existence. Once a spirit has become embodied, it is committed to living out the physical existence whether it likes it or not. There is no option in this. It is not just the law, but it is a basic fact. This life is the only life we can really be sure of. It is here. We are living it. "But," adds Master, "one can regulate one's life so as to *normalise* all the functions of the human system so that the person develops into a perfect human being." The word 'normalise' is most important in this context. One

does not aim, and is not expected to aim, at super-nor-
mal powers of the body which hatha yoga so lavishly
promises. Nor is one to aim at the attainment of *siddhis*
— such as the power to materialise objects, clair-
voyance, levitation and the like — for these too are not
normal to the human existence. I repeat, we are not to
'aim' for these in sadhana. Under the Sahaj Marg
method of yogic sadhana Master offers precisely this
training of how to normalise one's life in all the details
of its functions. Master has stated that most humans
start life as animals, and to humanise them becomes the
first step in sadhana. The animal man becomes a real
human by the practice of meditation which regulates
mental functions, and thereby makes it possible for the
regulation to percolate down to the physical level. It is
with the mind that we have to begin. Any process which
starts with the body is then obviously putting the cart
before the horse. Meditation is the abhyasi's part, the
part he has to play in this divine adventure. The
Master's work is to clean the abhyasi of past samskaras
and to transmit to him. I will not elaborate on this further as details are available in Master's published
works. One important aspect I would like to emphasise
is that there is no control of functions, or elimination of
any of them. All that is done is to seek to normalise
each and every function without atrophy of any of them.
Master bases his teaching on God's wisdom. God
created the universe. When he created a material
universe, He must have had good reason to do so. If the
material life is leading us astray and away from our goal,
then obviously it is our fault in not living the material
life in the appropriate fashion. So all that we have to do
to get back on to our path is to restore the proper
'balance' to our life whereby the two halves of existence

are harmonised and in equilibrium. The humanised man can then proceed to evolve to the state of the perfect human being.

Master is, as I said earlier, the living example of this way of life. He is a householder who has married and shouldered the arduous responsibilities of family life. He has experienced all the joys of love, and sorrows and miseries of separation that we suffer in our own narrower lives. It is surely a matter for wonder that he has so completely lived the life of the householder while simultaneously developing in himself the divine capacity to be a Master of spirituality too. His life is centred naturally around his own family. But whereas the centre and the circumference of our own lives have both merged into one single point which rests in the family, for Master the centre is the family while the circumference embraces the whole universe. This is the difference between his life and ours. And when Master, by his divine transmission, helps us to 'expand' into cosmic levels and super-cosmic levels of existence, he separates the shrunken circumference of our existence from its centre, setting the circumference free, or liberating it, so that it can expand wider and wider until it, in turn, is afforded the possibility of becoming universal. Thus, progressively, the individual self-centred human soul and consciousness develops and expands until it becomes a universal person possessing a universal consciousness similar to the Master himself.

Master was born in a well-to-do, well-known and highly respected family. His father was certainly rich by local standards. The family background is one of high culture and deep respect for traditions, the former nurtured by his father and the latter by his mother. Master, in turn, has led his own life on the very keel of these solid foundations laid down by his parents. Master's culture is so profound that it will not permit any undue or wanton criticism of other ways of life. To Master, everything has a place in the universal hierarchy. He teaches that other teachers are also doing God's work, each one at his own level. Tolerance, as taught by Master, is not a virtue but a definite duty enjoined on the abhyasi. No system can ascribe to itself exclusively either total importance or total effectiveness. If a mountain has a summit, it is because it has a base to support it!

Some of our abhyasis have spent very many years practising yoga under other systems of training. When they finally came to my Master, they were inclined to weep over their 'lost years,' lamenting the fact that they did not come to Master's feet earlier. Master's invariable advice is, "Do not regret the time spent on the other method. It was necessary for your development. It has prepared you for this path. Be joyful that you have now found the path that can lead you onward." Master teaches that while there are innumerable gurus, the real guru is none but God himself. It is the duty of each guru to lead his disciple to the next higher one when his own work with the disciple is finished. No guru should hold his disciples to himself possessively. A guru is for service to others and not for building up possessions, power and prestige for himself.

Tolerance must be extended to all facets of one's life. After many years of close personal association with my Master, I have come to the conclusion that tolerance is perhaps the most important spiritual quality as it seems to embrace, and emanate out of itself, the other virtues such as understanding, charity, and even love itself. I have often been told that love begets tolerance but, perhaps, the reverse that tolerance begets love, is true. It is an accepted psychological axiom that only those who have hatred for themselves in their hearts project the hatred on the world. Such hatred is self-hatred, and comes out of an inability to accept one's own qualities. In the widest understanding of the word, tolerance implies that everything has a place in the universal hierarchy, and it is the understanding of this basic truth of creation that tolerance reveals. Tolerance thus reveals the correct perspective in the universal scheme of things. We have been taught that good and evil co-exist, that they are nothing but different facets of the same reality. So too have we been taught to regard vice and virtue and all the other opposites of existence. Where one exists, the other must exist. There is no choice. Who, then, are we to revile at the negative (as we label them) manifestations? We are often haunted by the apparent antithesis in persons' characters — a rich man being miserly; an honest man indulging in secret thievery; a virtuous person having a hidden, seamy side to his existence; a religious person with a dark and unsavoury personal life. All this perturbs us and, what is worse, frustrates us in our search for knowledge and understanding. Tolerance can give us that quantum of time which will permit us to probe below the surface and see the underlying truth. This is a minimum benefit that tolerance confers — time to study and understand things. And inevitably when the externals are ignored and we penetrate deeper, then understanding, true understanding, comes and we find that persons are other than what they appear to be. If we are earnest in our endeavour and zealous in our pursuit, a time will surely come when we can see the saint inside the sinner! This, to my Master, is a permanent vision. He sees nothing but the true Reality within.

We were once discussing the presence in our satsangh of a person known to be highly immoral. Some abhyasis were wondering how such a person had been admitted for meditation. After considerable debate it was decided to approach Master for clarification. His answer was simple and direct. He said, "I do not look into the lower aspects. My eyes do not go there." He ignores all these things. Master sees what is best in a person, while we, at the ordinary human level, tend not only to see, but to look for, the worst. This is the difference.

To my personal knowledge Master has rarely criticised a person for anything. He also offers advice very very rarely. I asked Babuji once why he did not offer criticism when he saw something wrong. Babuji answered, "Lalaji Saheb never offered advice in a direct manner. Yes, he would give hints; but how many are capable of understanding such hints? We should never offer advice unless asked. As a trainer it is the duty of the guide to bring about change by creating the proper conditions for it. That is the work of the trainer. This is the positive approach. If you criticise, then the abhyasi may begin to worry about it, and this will interfere with his progress. There is another thing I am telling you. Suppose I advise an abhyasi to do something and he does not do it. Then I am adding to his difficulties by putting upon him the sin of disobedience of the Master. So instead of helping him I have done him a disservice. Do you understand why I avoid direct advice? I do offer a lot of advice, but it is given out as general talk when all are with me. The intelligent person will take it up and apply it in his own life. Then progress is faster for that person because now he is co-operating with the Master." We see from this that Master's attitude is not merely one of tolerance, but extends far beyond this to taking up responsibility for the abhyasi's progress. As Master has emphasised again and again, this is the duty of a trainer in spirituality.

I remember an episode a few years ago when I was sitting with Dr. K.C. Varadachari and several other abhyasis at his residence in Tirupathi. We had been talking for some time. A person, obviously a new abhyasi, entered the room and prostrated before Dr. Varadachari. He then sat close to him and started to talk to him. He was quite agitated. After some time he said, "Doctor, I am a miserable sinner." Dr. Varadachari became indignant. He asked in a voice of passionate emotion, "What sins have you committed? Some petty offense? A bottle of wine? A love affair? Come to me when you have done something original. Which fool has not committed these sins?" Later he became very soft and affectionate, and went on to calm the troubled soul of the abhyasi with his wise words.

The point I am trying to make is, what is so original about sin, and what is so unique about our own sins that we are ever preoccupied with them? Master teaches, very importantly and significantly, that there is no such thing as sin or virtue. All is samskara. Any action, whether it is good or bad, which forms impressions in the mind is creating a samskara and, in the spiritual sense, is undesirable. Sinning would appear to be certainly not as bad as the brooding over the sin, because brooding drives the impressions deeper and deeper into the mind, where samskaras of such hardness are formed that much subsequent effort is required to clean the system. Master advises us to forget the past. The past should not worry us because it **is** the past, and we can do nothing to change it. What should concern us is the future which we **can** affect by our present action. It is in this direction that our endeavours must lie. The immediate past is of no more consequence than the more distant past. "So," Master says, "think all past actions to be those of a past life. This will make it easy to ignore them and to concentrate on laying the basis for future spiritual development." This is an important teaching to us as abhyasis.

How does prejudice develop? How do we evaluate a person's character? By what are we conditioned in our interpersonal relationships? The answer to all these questions is that a man's antecedents are what guide us. If we can develop the ability to look on a person at this instant as a fresh, unknown entity, unconditioned by any past, then we will develop the capacity to see the real person, and not merely the external, tortured, human being that everybody sees. Then an objective ability develops, which penetrates beyond the external veils and sees the truth within. A person's past may have been anything. What is he now? This is the most important thing. But we, most of us, rarely ask this question because we are preeminently worried only about the past antecedents. Thus we miss the real person and see only a tangled and superficial web of trivialities enclosing the individual like a fly in a spider's web. That is why all new acquaintances are so glamorous, so welcome, while old friends are the ones with whom we quarrel and from whom we often part. Living in the present unites us, while living in the past can tend to separate person from person and, as history records for us, even nation from nation.

Prospective entrants to this system invariably ask one question. "What are the qualifications required to be a member of this system?" Master's only answer to this question is, "Your willingness is the only qualification needed." And invariably people wonder how this can be so. An element of ego is also present in this bewilderment. After all, who wants to join an association of persons where such an apparently trivial qualification is all that is needed? Before we get into an organisation we like it to be as easy as possible. But if it is too easy doubt begins to emerge as to the worthiness of the organisation. Also, we like barriers to be just large enough to enable us to cross over into the chosen ground comfortably, but sufficiently large to keep out the rabble. But in a yogic system where the **present** is the only criterion, what other qualities can there possibly be which are important? Willingness alone is in the present. All else, breeding, education, qualifications are over and done with. They have limitations and, in any case, do not last forever. They serve merely to lay foundations. Willingness denotes a very important mental state. It indicates that a person has evaluated himself and sees the need for change, and that he is prepared to act to bring about such change. So persons with this state of mind are ready to act and, more importantly, to be acted upon. They are the real raw material for Master's work. In thus defining the necessary qualifications, Master does no more than voice this inner truth. He once told a visitor, "What you have been is of no importance. What is the use if your grandfather was a maharaja, but you are a beggar now? It would have been better if your grandfather had been a beggar and you a maharaja. So try to see what you can do to grow in yourself. For this you must begin now. And I am prepared to help you!" Thus, at one stroke, Master destroys the edifice of social snobbery by saying class is unimportant, social eminence is unimportant and alas! even education is unnecessary. All that is essential for success is contained in the abhyasis' willingness to accept guidance from the Master, and to pursue the path inexorably.

If we examine this concept of 'willingness' carefully we find that ultimately it points to the need for total surrender to the Master. As Master has repeatedly emphasised, surrender is necessary on the part of the abhyasi if Master's work is to succeed. In one of Master's writings he has given a pointer to this. What should be the ideal abhyasi's attitude? In Master's own words, "He must be like a dead man in the hands of the dresser." That is, the abhyasi must be like a corpse, devoid of personal desire, personal opinions, and completely denuded of all resistance. Such an abhyasi is ideal material as he offers no resistance whatsoever, either physical or mental, to Master's spiritual powers. Master has used another illustration to emphasise this point. He has stated that a carpenter can easily fashion whatever he desires from timber, but if he is given a chair as raw material to work with, what can he do? With timber he is free to do as he pleases, and to fashion what he has decided to create, whereas with a chair he is faced with severe limitations which cannot generally be overcome.

Once Master clarified this point with a third illustration. What do we do when we go to a doctor for treatment? We accept all that he says. We abide by his regimen of diet and medication. We follow his prescription on what we are to do and what we are to abstain from doing. If surgery is necessary we allow ourselves to be anaesthetized into a totally inactive condition so as to permit him to operate upon us. We have to do all this if the doctor is to succeed in helping us. Does this not imply a surrender to the doctor's will and method? Can we question his method? Can we ask for a guarantee of success? Yet without all this we are prepared to surrender ourselves to the will of the doctor. Why, then, cannot we duplicate this attitude in our spiritual life? In spiritual life we ask for proofs first — proof of the existence of God, let us say; proof of the system's efficacy, and so on. Master said this was not only wrong but illogical. Master added, "Suppose I am willing to offer proof, how many can understand the proof? Look here, suppose you ask a scientist to prove certain abstract ideas, how many can understand the proof? And the higher the work the more difficult it is to understand the subject. So we should try the system, and our own experience of the work will furnish the proof from within ourselves."

There is another very vital point to be considered in Master's offer of help and guidance. He merely asks for willingness, forgetting all the past thoughts and deeds of the abhyasi. Why? Precisely because it is past. The abhyasi can do nothing about his own past. We are literally the products of our past, but we are **not** the mute and impotent participants in our future which we assume ourselves to be. The past has brought us to the present. Beyond this it has no power to act. The future will be what we make of it now, in the present. So, by changing our way of life **now** the future can be changed. Master therefore teaches us not to think of the past at all, but only to think, and more importantly to act, in the present. Extending the medical analogy, the doctor looks into the past merely to seek causes for present illness. His action, remedial, healing and creative, is in the present. There is no use in a doctor blaming the patient for the past actions which have brought on the present illness. A doctor worth his name studies the patient and quietly goes on with his task of healing. This is what Master does in his spiritual work. Our past may be important to him, but to us it has no importance. On the contrary our brooding about the past will only serve to strengthen our impressions and drive them in deeper and deeper, forming solid samskaras which are more difficult to clean. Herein lies the vital importance of surrendering up our past to Master, and forgetting it, but living the present as he guides us, so that our future can be what he wills it to be.

All that we consider desirable and covet are thus thrown on the dust heap, and we are asked to make a new beginning in which we come to Master as a soul entombed in a human body, seeking the highest goal open to mankind. Immediately and miraculously the possibility is opened up of creating a brotherhood of man where all that is asked of us is that we be human beings. As Master destroys the false edifices man has created around himself, of power, wealth, eminence, education and so on, we too are required to destroy all this in our own mentalities. What he does, we in turn must do. What is thrown to the winds must be thrown away once and for all. So this great tolerance for mankind as a whole, and for each of its units as a human being, is inculcated and practised. And in thus reducing all human-kind to its grass-roots, Master is most benevolent and god-like. This is the greatest gift of his divine wisdom where, to the creator, all are one. Can a man differentiate between individual ants in an ant hill? To us all ants appear the same. Perhaps they have a government, a social structure, a class stratification, but to us all this is non-existent. How much more must we humans all look alike to a Godly vision from above! When we emulate Master and learn to see all as one, then we too aspire to this godly conscience, to the development of such a divine consciousness in us, and the mere aspiration lifts us up and opens up the possibility of its actualisation.

So, coming back to tolerance, we see and understand how it is not merely one of the virtues, but is the cardinal virtue; and not merely this, it is the perception of the truth of creation that all men are created equal in God's vision, and we do nothing but destroy the basic value of such creation when we seek to classify and divide what has been created as one. So tolerance is conforming to God's intent and design, and such conformity enables us to swim in the same direction as the current, thus making our journey not only trouble-free but doubly fast. In this lies the possibility of a speedy evolution to our goal within this life itself.

The ultimate benefit of this training is that a person is able to see himself as he really is, shorn of all attributes; and the ability to live with oneself develops as we grow to like what we see. After all, which of us really knows himself? But to know oneself one has perhaps to start by knowing and understanding others. Then this trained gaze must be turned from outwards inside. And as we see human beings swayed hither and thither by their attributes, we gain a deep insight and understanding of the mysteries of existence, followed by a tenderness and love which develop spontaneously from such a deeper understanding. Then there is no revulsion, no abhorrence, no villification — because all is as it should be, so long as men and women continue to be

as they are. Here begins to dawn the wisdom which says
that all change must begin with oneself. As I change and
grow, so does my vision, my consciousness. And with
this growth a parallel possibility is given, that of helping
others to strive for and achieve change and progress in
themselves. So, all reform must begin, like charity, at
home.

The traditional or familiar type of reformer who
raves at a patient and long-suffering public, preaching
hell-fire and damnation, is merely raving against himself, but using the public as a vicarious target. The true
reformer is a silent worker who preaches against nothing, who reviles nothing, and who condemns no one but,
having worked upon himself silently and in secret, sets
out to do the same with and for others, in the same
secret and silent manner. This is how my Master works,
silently, without publicity and propaganda. His work is
backed by Nature's infinite resources of power and wisdom which have been placed at his command without
reserve.

IV
Duty

Master's interpretation of such concepts as charity, renunciation and duty is radically different from the usual ideas or meanings attached to them. We all think we know what they mean. Indeed our familiarity with these ideas is so thorough that we would be astonished if someone told us we do not know what these terms really mean. Most persons have the feeling that they have also been practising these ideas in accordance with the dictates of society and religion, occasionally of conscience too. And our own understanding so coincides with that of those around us that it is difficult to see how there could possibly be any other way of understanding these ideas. In any case we continue to do as we have always done, in the confidence that we have the religious tenets to back us up.

We are all familiar with the institution of religious charity, which I would call 'ritual charity,' practised by well-meaning men and women all over the world, whatever be their religious affiliation. The coin in the plate or special receptacle! Donations towards special causes thought up by pious persons; offerings in kind, all these are only too familiar to us. Then there is the coin dropped into the hands of a beggar outside the place of worship. Such charity is held to be a pious act, capable of elevating the giver, and earning for him the blessings of the Almighty. Eastern religions are beset by this apparent virtue to a greater extent than their European counterparts.

What does the giver give away? Often it is nothing but a single copper coin of the lowest denomination, and that too generally to the accompaniment of admonitions and chastisement of the poor beggar for being a beggar. When this gift, supposedly prescribed by religion, has been bestowed, the donor's face glows with a self-righteous glow at having fulfilled religion's behest. Often this is the first of a series of expiatory and propitiatory acts when entering the place of worship. Another aspect of such charity is to give away left-over food. It would be laudable if this was done while the food was still edible, but the charitable individual, in general, prefers to ensure that he is not depriving his family. So the left-overs are left over till nobody can eat them, and then, and then only, is the food given away to a poor beggar who is too starved to worry about the quality of what he eats. Again this charitable act is accompanied by much good and pious advice, and very often by abuse too.

Then there are the gifts given to abide by the advice of astrologers. Such gifts can often be very expensive depending on the degree to which certain planets are afflicted. In such cases the gift of jewels, silks, silver vessels etc. are made to other members of the family circle and not to really needy persons. This is designed to spend money while keeping it within the family. There are also instances of what I call, for lack of a better term, the 'final' hypocrisy. This applies in the case of individuals embarking on the most pious and righteous act of renouncing all wealth and possessions, preparatory to entering the holy state of *sannyasa*. In rare cases, certain individuals do give away their wealth to the needy, but more often such people apportion their wealth suitably among their kith and kin before donning the yellow robes. This, too, is charity! Many sannyasis go on earning 'gifts' and 'donations' which they send back to their erstwhile families. In such cases, not rare or uncommon by any means, the sannyasi often becomes a better provider than in his former incompetent role of householder.

I am not giving these examples to criticise existing ideas or to decry existing practices. After all, people can only behave as they are taught to behave. And when such teaching is the product of religious thought and precepts as interpreted by the care-takers of religion, the priests, there is very little people can do but obey blindly. The majority of mankind know no better than to superstitiously follow the instructions of the religious scriptures as interpreted by the priesthood. Superstition, and the fear it generates, are the compelling causes underlying such charitable acts. If people could be made to see the light of truth and shed superstition, much of this religious hypocrisy would automatically vanish. In India religion has a firm and tenacious hold on an individual's life, and almost all aspects of life from birth to the final disposal of the dead are governed by rules of ritual and procedure. The interests of the priests, who officiate at each and every one of these ceremonies, whether for the living or for the dead, are zealously guarded by prescribing fees at each stage of the ritual, euphemistically called 'offerings.' In such a society the people have no choice but to suffer in silence and part, outwardly cheerfully, with a portion of their hard-earned income. The more hardy and experienced individuals bargain with the priesthood to limit their loss while making the ritual as all-embracing as possible, while the meek suffer the most. The only compensation these poor sufferers have is that of put-

ting on a virtuous face — which they do to the best of
their ability!

After saying all this I must, in fairness to all
religions, add that religions themselves are not responsible for this state of affairs. All this is nothing but the
rapacious hold that a greedy priesthood has on a very
gullible and illiterate public as we have in India.

What does my Master teach about these matters?
Firstly, no person has a right to indulge in charity until
his family needs are fully satisfied. No person has a
right to give away money or gifts until he has made absolutely sure that such gifts are coming out of available
surplus in the family's means of existence. Otherwise it
is merely a case of robbing Peter to pay Paul. On superficial examination this looks to be a very very selfish
approach. I had a long discussion with Master on this
once. Master said, "Look! suppose you want to give
away a sum of money as charity, and your family will suffer because of it, can you call this charity? I would only
call it foolishness. What is your duty as a *grihastha*
(householder)? When you married and accepted the
responsibilities of a family existence, you accepted to
fulfill certain duties by the family. These duties are totally obligatory. Therefore, if your gift is going to make
the family suffer, then it is not a gift at all, it is not
charity. You are really robbing your own family. Look
here! How can this robbery be called charity." I then
asked Master whether such an act of charity would be
justified if the other members of the family agreed to it.
Master answered, "No! It cannot make it right. Which
Hindu wife will go against her husband's wishes? And
in the case of religious performances or ceremonies
they will not oppose it. It is for you to decide what is
your duty, and then it is your duty to follow that correct-

ly. If you consult others you are only trying to shift the blame and responsibility on others." I asked a third question. What about the negligible gifts made to beggars etc.? Master laughed an ironical laugh. "Do you call it charity?" he asked. "To feed the poor and to give some rags to your brother human beings is not charity. It is your duty. It is our duty as human beings to look after our suffering brothers and sisters. It is a shame that this is thought to be charity." This dialogue made it amply clear that unless a person can really afford a gift, he has no right to make one in any form. Master's interpretation is from the standpoint of duty.

It is an anomalous fact that poor people often seem to be able to afford more for charity than rich people. The sacrifices that poor people have made not only during normal times but during times of national disaster, natural calamities and so on is something to be wondered at. Master's interpretation which differentiates need from want explains this curious anomaly. Master, in my experience, has never used the word 'want' but always sticks to the use of the word 'needs.' This emphasises the fact that there is a basic difference between the two terms. Needs are basic to existence, whereas wants are those which are created by desires, and superfluous in one way or the other to existence. This is why poor people are able to afford charity because their needs are very few, since their lives are simple and in tune with nature. Therefore, however small their income, and however low their level of existence, it seems to be possible for them always to scrape up some quantum of surplus from their own existence which they can offer whole-heartedly to alleviate the miseries of their brother human beings. In the case of the rich, who are burdened with what is sophisticatedly called higher standards of living, the wants are enormous in terms of luxury, in terms of unnecessary paraphernalia so that whatever be their level of income they seem always to need more and more money to meet the expenses created by yet new desires, and this goes on *ad infinitum*. When this has gone on sufficiently, some of the rich often start feeling guilty, and then it is not uncommon to find a few of them giving large amounts to charity. But their mind is so befogged that often the money is wasted on conscience-placating ventures like building temples, rather than in helping the poorer section of humanity to live a better life. Such persons often waste their enormous wealth in doing what they consider to be charitable acts. It is common for them to turn away a beggar from their door while, under priestly instructions, being willing to spend minor fortunes on a single occasion in placating their family deities. It is rare to find an inner change in such individuals which will lead them to the right path. Their fear of retribution for the evils committed becomes merely a superstitious force driving them from pillar to post in a religious way of ritual propitiation. There is no change of heart but merely a fear-motivated unburdening of ill-gotten wealth, similar to the frantic bailing out of water from a sinking boat. If the rich would simplify their lives in accordance with Master's basic teachings, the surplus that would be released would be simply enormous. We find the same law working even at international levels where certain nations are saturated with economic abundance but are yet unwilling, and often unable, to divert their surplus to the more needy nations. This calls for universal understanding by all human beings as to how to guide their individual lives in such a way that the gifts of nature's bounty are made available to all rather than to a mere few. I remember a discussion in a Western capital which centred on the issue of lowering birth rates in underdeveloped countries. Some well-meaning friends were trying to prove that if only countries like India would drastically reduce their populations, then the land would flow with milk and honey. The argument came to a rather abrupt end when an Indian gentleman present pointed out that a UN Commission report had given statistics to show that the amount spent on bringing up a Western baby in the first year would suffice to feed and bring up 500 babies in an underdeveloped nation. This points to the gross over-consumption by Western nations, and the need for such people to curb consumption if the people of the world, as a whole, are to benefit from available world resources. A significant fact worth noticing is that poverty creates charity whereas affluence breeds self-ishness.

Master strictly enforces this with his abhyasis too. I have seen him time and again refusing to accept donations offered by his abhyasis. He invariably asks the abhyasi, "Where are you working? What do you earn? Are you married? How many dependents have you?" And after all this, if the answers satisfy him, he may accept the donation. In certain cases he has refused donations even after all this clarification. I asked him why he refused certain donations. He said, "Some people sincerely want to help the Mission. If they can really afford it then I accept what they give. There are others who offer me a donation only to impress me with their generosity (laughing). The donation does not come from the heart but only from the purse. In such cases I refuse it." To Master a donation by itself means nothing. He cares nothing for the money. But it is an indication of the abhyasi's love for Master and the Mission. Master therefore accepts donations only as tokens of the love of the donor. I have known Master refusing really large donations on two occasions. The amounts offered were so very large that a lesser person than Master would have instantly accepted them. On the other hand I have known Master to be deeply moved when an abhyasi, with tears in her eyes, offered very humbly, shyly and with great hesitation, an incredibly small amount as a donation. Master was overjoyed with the offering and instantly accepted it, and kept on talking about it to everyone for months. I asked him why he made such a fuss over such a small amount. Master said, "If Birla were to give me a crore of rupees it would be as nothing to Birla, because it is a small fraction of his wealth. But what this abhyasi has given, though such a tiny amount, has been laboriously saved over many months, and represents the entire savings of the abhyasi. You see the degree of sacrifice, and the love behind it? Therefore I value it greatly."

Once at Shahjahanpur an old man, aged more than 70, came to see Master. He was quite active, well dressed and with an enormous turban wound round his head. Master agreed to meet him and give him some time. Master set the conversational ball rolling by asking him where he was from, and what he did. The person answered that he was from a nearby town and that he was a social worker. Master said, "Is that so! I am very happy to hear that you are a social worker. It is what our country needs. What do you actually do?" The aged person was gratified to have this reaction, and said that he organised meetings in villages where he distributed clothes to the needy, and also did mass poorfeeding. Master said, "Oh! You call this social service?

This is not correct. As a human being it is your duty to your brothers and sisters to clothe the naked and feed the hungry. It is unfortunate that you should call this social service. The real social service is not this. When you can do something to raise up your brothers and sisters to the true goal of realisation, then that can be called social service." After this person left, Master remarked to me, "See how our values have degenerated. Our country has always been known for its spiritual values and for the great hospitality of our people. But now this is what we have become. But still I am telling you, nowhere in the world will you find such hospitality as you find in India, even today. By Lalaji's Grace India will rise again to be the spiritual leader of mankind."

In Master's own household one can see his principles being applied exactly. It is an instruction in itself to observe how Master is the living example of his own teaching. The accommodation provided for visitors is of the simplest, while being comfortable. Luxury is not provided. Similarly, the food offered to visitors is wholesome and nourishing but of the simplest variety. There is no ostentation, no impressive variety, and no pandering to taste. I have found that this is akin to Nature's way of service. Such food helps us to get what we need from it, nourishment, and prevents greediness and over-indulgence. Taste, artificially created taste, only creates greed and leads to unnatural living. Simple food helps us to live as Nature intended us to live, eating what the body needs for its healthy existence and no more. This is a very valuable lesson which Master teaches us by direct example.

Once at lunch at Shahjahanpur, one of the abhyasis was very critical of the quality of the food, and particularly the monotonous repetition of the same preparations day after day. He was quite vocal in his criticism. He said he wished there would be some variety in the menu, and wondered why something could not be done to make the food more tasty and appetising. After completing lunch we all came out of the room and went to the verandah where Master was sitting in his usual easy-chair. Master could not possibly have heard the abhyasi's remarks. Yet, as soon as we came near him, Master got up from his chair, walked a few steps to meet us, and told the disgruntled abhyasi, "Look here! I give simple food for the body but I give Divine food for the Soul!" He then went back to his chair and his hookah. A few minutes later I chanced to be alone with him, and Master said, "Look what people expect of me. I have told them that I can take complete responsibility for their soul, but the body they must look after themselves. I try to give good food. We must eat enough to keep the body fit to take us through life. Food is not for taste, it is only for nourishment. I think I give good food, enough for this purpose. I am here to serve people for their spiritual needs, but if they think I am here to provide tasty feasts for them too, then what can I do."

Many families have been ruined by putting up a false front on borrowed money. Ego is the cause of such behaviour. We live and entertain beyond our means merely to impress others in our circle. But good opinion, so bought, is very very expensive, and one has to pay for it bitterly in the end. True seekers of Reality cannot indulge in such hypocritical behaviour. We must take Master as our living example and conduct our lives as he does his.

Ever since the Mission was founded in 1945 there has been a steady influx of visitors into Shahjahanpur.

In the beginning it was but a trickle. Now, with the growth and expansion of the Mission, the trickle has become a flood. And yet, all these years Master has been entertaining his guests out of his own personal resources. His resources have always been very slender. How he has been able to feed the thousands of visitors who go to see him each year, and often clothe quite a few of them too, is a matter for wonder. Those who know him know that while in service he occupied a humble position in life, one which could hardly have offered any scope for savings of any magnitude. But by studying his way of living it is clear that if we can simplify our lives, and eschew all ostentation, all unnecessary paraphernalia and luxury, then even a small income can be made to stretch a very long way. Master's call to modern humanity is, "Be simple and in tune with Nature." He lives the life that he asks others to live. Master considers all artificial ways of living as unnecessary, harmful and often hypocritical. Our hospitality must be geared to our means. Hospitality, flamboyant hospitality on borrowed money, can only be hypocritical as it seeks to impress others, and is untrue and unreal and opposed to Reality. This is a moral lesson which we need to learn and to disseminate.

I have had long discussions with Master on one condition most religions seem to prescribe: to give away all wealth and property before embarking on a religious way of life. Some even prescribe total renunciation of the family, and adoption of asceticism. Master is quite definite that such prescriptions are unnecessary, and some may even go against Nature. He said, "What is wrong with wealth as long as it is rightly earned? When a man works he is entitled to the fruit of his labour. Yes! There is a right way of using wealth, as there are innumerable wrong ways. Wealth is only a power. And all power is good so long as it is used constructively for the good of humanity. Every person has a right to earn money lawfully. I see nothing wrong in it. But we must not be **attached** to wealth. It must not become the aim. Our Goal must always be fixed, and there must be no straying from it. Anything may come on the way, but we must go on and on towards our goal. You must treat wealth like a river. Take as much of it as you need, and then use the rest for the benefit of your brothers and sisters. That is the right way. Now look here! They say you must leave your family and children and run away to the jungle, or to the Himalayas. What is the use? It is not easy to do it. It is against Nature. It is also a cowardly act as you are running away from your duties and responsibilities. When you are in the jungle your thoughts will be only of the home and family. How can you do tapasya under such conditions? Then what is the correct way? I am telling you it is better to bring the jungle into your home, rather than carry your home into the jungle. How is this to be done? Really speaking it is quite simple. Think that in your own home you are only a guest. You will find all problems evaporate. Treat your wife and children as trust property entrusted to you by God. They are not yours. They are not your wife and not your children, but they are under your trust, under your care. You understand this? All sense of possession must go. It is only when you think 'this thing is mine' that loss also comes. When it is in trust you can administer it objectively and very correctly. You will be able to do for them what they need, what is necessary. Really speaking you learn correct performance of duty only in the family environment. Lalaji used to say that the *grihastha* life is the most important training ground, for it is here that we learn true charity, true love, true renunciation. Only in the life of the householder do we learn to think of others before we think of ourselves. So it is very important. And I tell you it is really very easy. Just divert the mind!"

Master continued, "Really speaking I have not much opinion about *sannyasa*. Yes, there are a few genuine sannyasis who have adopted that way of life out of a true and genuine spirit of renunciation and longing for the Divine. But the majority are only those who have run away from the responsibilities of life and are living off society. Some of them are quite bad too in their ways of life and moral behaviour. But our people have been taught to revere them, and many suffer for it."

According to Master the ancient traditional ways of renunciation of wealth and family can be exceedingly harmful, spiritually, and can block an abhyasi's spiritual progress, sometimes through several lives. I was told the spiritual case history of an abhyasi under Master who had been practicing Sahaj Marg meditation for nearly 15 years. However the person had stagnated at one point, and all progress had stopped there. Master had made several attempts to initiate further progress but had not been successful. At this stage Master decided to examine the abhyasi's past life and see whether there was some cause there preventing progress in the present life. Master examined the past life during a special meditation sitting. He found that in the previous life this abhyasi had been a woman, married and with several children. She was a lady of deep devotion and sincerely desired to pursue the ancient goal of obtaining *mukti*, a limited form of liberation under which there is no physical rebirth. She had felt irked at having to lead the life of a housewife. Being desirous of adopting *sannyasa*, she one day stole away from her home with her children, took them into the jungle, and abandoned them on the bank of a river there. Then she ran away. The frightened children set up a wailing which followed her as she ran away. Unable to hear their lament, she closed her ears with the palms of her hands and ran on and on. Master found that the wailing of the abandoned children had created a very strong and profound impression on the mind, leading to the formation of deep *samskaras*. This had prevented spiritual progress of the abhyasi in the present life. Master said, "Look here! She thought she had done a virtuous thing which would earn her *mukti*, but really it was a cruel and heartless act. So Nature punished her in this life by denying spiritual progress, the very thing for which she renounced her family life!" Then he added, "Since the abhyasi is very sincere and has real craving for progress, I cut that impression. Do you know what happened? The person immediately moved up three points! I call this spirituality. It is Lalaji's Grace that this is possible. Where can one find a Master like Him! But for Lalaji's Grace I do not know how many more lives that poor woman would have had to take before she could move forward. **We must not go against Nature.** See how much evil has been spread by people who know nothing. I tell you, unless these wrong ways of approach are given up spirituality is impossible."

This case history has profound implications for us. Asceticism is NOT the right way. It is as wrong, and as anti-nature, as a totally materialistic way of life is. They are but two extremes of the scale, and neither can succeed. Then what is the correct way? Master says that the balanced existence, one in which all aspects of human existence are balanced, is the only correct way of life. In such a life material values and spiritual values go side by side, and one should not be neglected for the other. We must devote equal attention to both sides of existence. The two sides of existence are like the two wings of a bird. No bird can fly on one wing. It needs both. Similarly we have to live both the material and spiritual existences in a balanced way, using them as instruments to take us to our Goal. They should not become ends in themselves. Some persons make the mistake of taking the spiritual life or pursuit to be an end in itself. It is only a means to an end. Our goal must be a fixed and definite one, that of achieving the perfect human condition. In this there must be no wavering, no faltering. The material life, the life of and in the body, offers the possibility of seeking and attaining this goal. So, to that extent, our life in the body is essential. It is in **this** life, in **this** existence that we can and must seek our goal. The spiritual life too, is merely the way to be trodden, and not to be mistaken for the goal. It is in this confusion of the way for the Goal that much human misery lies. It is also the failure of religion, because a religious or pious life, by itself, is incapable of leading us to the goal. When people mistake the way for the goal then life becomes meaningless, and ritualistic and mechanical. Then stagnation sets in, in the individual, in society, and in a whole nation. Master repeatedly emphasises this crucial aspect of his system, that the two sides of life, the material and the spiritual, are both necessary to help us reach our spiritual destination, and the degree to which they can be normalised and balanced will determine the degree of our success. I have referred certain personal problems to Master, seeking his guidance to achieve perfect balance. Master's reply was terse but illuminating. "Perfect balance cannot be achieved in the human existence. If perfect balance is achieved then this life will end immediately. We must aim for proper functioning of all our faculties. This is itself a great thing. Such proper functioning of all our faculties I call saintliness. Perfect balance can exist only in Him!"

In India we have been hearing a great deal about non-violence all of our lives. Non-violence, or *ahimsa* as it is termed in Sanskrit, would appear to be one of the vital aspects of Hindu *dharma*. One of the important statements relating to this says *ahimsa paramodharmaha*, non-violence is the highest duty. In one of the religions this practice of non-violence is carried to the extent of walking bare-foot so as not to crush any insect life under the feet, and pads are used to cover the mouth and nostrils so that life-forms carried in air should not be breathed in and destroyed inside our system. The enormous number of useless cattle to be found all over India also endorses the widespread practice of this system. But there are curious reservations in this practice. The *ahimsa* practised is not a universal *ahimsa*. That is, it does not embrace within its scope all life, but only those selected for protection by the religion concerned. To Hindus the cow is sacred, so the cow should not be slaughtered. Sometimes the question of cow slaughter assumes such exaggerated importance and publicity that it gets blown up into a national debate, with political and religious leaders joining in the fray. But the same protagonists of *ahimsa* are prepared to destroy, with violent gusto, other life-forms for which they have no regard. There is a deep antithesis between precept and practice. And unfortunately the *ahimsa* principle seems to find no place in interpersonal relations at the human level. Tragic and ignominious examples of this

crass and inhuman disregard for life can be found in the
wanton and wilful destruction of hundreds of thousands
of innocent human lives during inter-religious or inter-
communal feuds.

I have had occasion to discuss this question of *ahimsa* with Master, and his explanation, as always, is very
simple and easy to accept. Wanton destruction is *himsa*
or violence. I asked for clarification. Master laughed
and said, "Suppose you are going out at night and you
have some money in one pocket, and some more in
another. A thief holds you up with a gun or knife and
asks you to give up your money. You take out money
from one pocket and give it to him. He, being afraid of
coming too near you, asks you if you have any more.
Will you say "yes" and give him the money from your
other pocket? Certainly that would be very foolish.
Why? Because your duty is to protect your possessions,
and anything you do to protect them is right. Suppose
somebody comes violently into your house, some
rowdy, and tries to molest the women of the house. Will
you keep quiet and practise *ahimsa*? That is only
cowardice. Your duty is to protect those for whom you
are responsible, and if you have to beat him and throw
him out, it must be done. I would say this must be
looked at from the point of view of duty alone. Doing
your duty is right conduct, *dharma*. I am telling you one
thing. This idea of *ahimsa* is a good idea, but if it is applied wrongly it can make people weak and impotent.
How can soldiers practise non-violence? It is their duty
to kill the enemy. In the *Gita* Sri Krishna tells Arjuna
the same thing. He tells him to go and destroy the
enemy, otherwise it is cowardice. Take the case of a
doctor. When he cures a sick man he does it by destroying the germs in the body. Strictly speaking this is

violence too, but would anyone be prepared to die to save germs? (Laughing.) We have to see what the destruction is for, whether it is necessary for correct performance of duty; for creation. Restoration of health is a creative act. There can be no creation without destruction. So destruction is not wrong or bad in itself. The motive behind it is what is to be examined. In the mind there must be no destructive thought or emotion. That is bad. A soldier kills impersonally. He does not know whom he is killing. He has no hatred in his heart for the individual he kills. His actions are not motivated by personal greed or hatred. He is merely doing his duty. Similarly a doctor has no hatred in his heart for the germs which he destroys. But to preserve life he has to do it. Suppose a snake comes to bite your child, will you keep quiet? Such *ahimsa* is mere foolishness.

"In spirituality obedience is the highest virtue. When a person surrenders to a Master, it means he has surrendered completely in all ways. He has become merely an instrument in the Master's hands. How can such a person even try to decide what is right or wrong? Here obedience alone is correct. There are various levels of existence, and duty is different from level to level. The soldier obeys the captain's orders; but in ordering his troops the captain, in turn, is only obeying the orders of his immediate superior officer — and this goes on up the scale of authority. In spiritual work there is no question of personal preferences or of personal opinions. The Master guides us in all ways. And if Nature wants destruction, it has to be carried out. We are merely instruments. If one instrument turns out to be blunt and useless, the craftsman will throw it away and take up a better one. You understand this idea? So obedience is the highest virtue. After all Master, who works for Nature and carries out the orders from above, knows what is to be done." On this note the discussion ended.

At a subsequent discussion session both the topics of obedience and destruction were again raised by me. I asked Master why sincere people should be blamed for obeying the religious teachers. After all they were only doing what Master himself was saying was most important. They were obeying their preceptors. Master agreed that there was some justification in thinking like this. He however added something which made this subject very clear. He said, "Obedience is good. I agree they obey, maybe only partly, yet the spirit of obedience is there. But I tell you, suppose they obey a dacoit, is it correct? No, it cannot be. A dacoit destroys life only to loot the wealth of the people. There is no other motive behind it. Similarly people may obey others who tell them to do something or other. Behind all this obedience there is only the selfish greed for personal gain. Why do people make large offerings to priests or astrologers? It is only for personal gain. So this is one thing, one aspect. Secondly, there may be sincere people who obey without any selfish desires. In their case what is the fault? You will find some highly sincere and loyal chelas with even robbers and dacoits. They almost worship them. Why is this? It is because they have not come to any judgment regarding the person they have become attached to. I have written in *Reality at Dawn* about the importance of seeking the right guru. If you obey the right guru it is good and will lead you to your goal. But if you have the wrong person to guide you then obedience will not help you at all. So you see the importance of having the right guru? In my opinion this is the most important thing, to find the real Master. Then when you find him you should never let him go! If you don't find such a Master then it is better to pray to God to send you a real Master. He will surely come. But there must be no compromise in this matter. I tell you it is better to have no guru at all than to have the wrong guru. Without a real Master we may not move forwards, but it is better than going backwards with the wrong guru. So I tell my associates we must be very careful in this matter. It is very vital. People ask me how they can judge a Master. It is easy. Your heart will give you the answer. I have told you that when you sit near a real saint you must feel peace. This is one sign. If you find a person who you think can guide you, then follow his teaching for some time sincerely. Continue if you find progress. If not, look for another guide. People have been taught that we cannot change our guide. But this is not correct. We take a guide for our benefit, not his. And we have every right to change the guide until we find the real Master. Then our job is over. Once you have handed yourself over to such a person, your work is over."

I then reverted to the subject of destruction which had been worrying me somewhat. I asked Master how destruction could ever be justified. Master answered, "Yes, you have some doubt. But it is there only because you are thinking in a narrow way. Think of destruction as change. What happens when you cut down a tree? The tree is destroyed. But the carpenter makes furniture out of it. So the wood is used. The wood is still there, the form has changed. When a person dies we think it is the end. Death is final, that is our view. But it is not correct. What we see as death is only the rebirth into another life. Similarly what we see as birth, when a baby is born, must be death in another life giving birth here. You understand this? It is only a change of form. The life goes on and on, but the form keeps changing until a fortunate person finds a Master who can grant him his liberation. This comes out of higher understanding. There can be no progress without change. Without change there is only stagnation. This is an important point I am telling you. Without change no progress is possible."

Master then added something very important for the clarification of our abhyasis. He said, "Even in our abhyas we must remember this. The condition, that is the spiritual condition, must keep changing if there is progress. Often we find that an abhyasi has a good experience at a particular level, which he likes to be repeated at subsequent sittings. But I always tell them that if they have the same experience again and again, then they should run to the preceptor, because such repetition of experience shows stagnation, and requires correction. So change is necessary because without it no progress is possible."

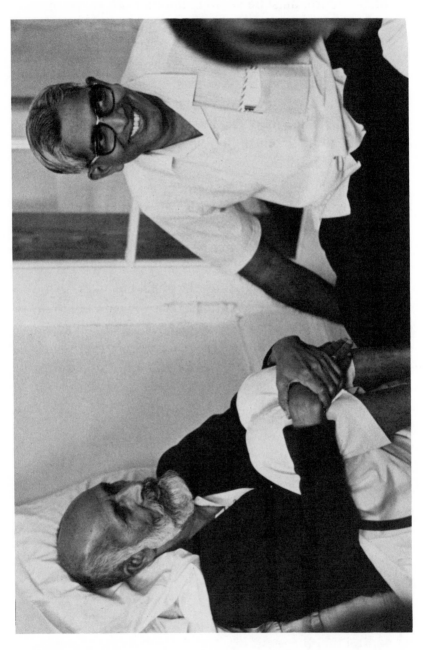

Babuji and the author

V

Love

All religions preach Love. It has formed the major theme of the world's output of great poetry. At the individual level everyone seeks it in his or her own life. Love has been responsible for heroic deeds, for acts of great courage and valour, and for much of the world's artistic output. It is probably quite true to say that behind every act of human endeavour lies this search for love. And its glorious working of unsurpassed beauty is in the manifestation of faith — faith at all levels culminating in the spiritual life where love finds its supreme flowering and glory in the search for the unknown Ultimate.

My Master too frequently refers to the need for love in one's life. One of his most revealing ideas is that love is a godly or divine thing, and therefore not to be spurned. Love is to be diverted to its proper and natural object, God! What the human individual is required to do is to divert his mind so that the love in the heart can be diverted to its real goal.

My Master's personal life is the expression of his inner love for all mankind. His is a pure and divine love, universal in its scope and yet individual in its manifestation. Anyone who has closely observed Master would have found, as I have, that he is the most loving, charitable and hospitable person one can find. He is all this, but in a manner so quiet, so subdued and so utterly natural that the significance of his actions are generally lost in their simplicity. Few onlookers penetrate his external simplicity to perceive the inner significance of his words and acts. In fact Master's simplicity is highly deceptive — and the only thing about him that deceives people. Once when Master was talking to one of our overseas preceptors he said, "Look here, I never deceive anybody, but what can I do if they deceive themselves? My simplicity is the thing that deceives most people. Few persons are able to go beyond it. My simplicity is so much that all my life people have thought me to be a simpleton." Master laughed when he said this, and continued, "Now look here, many people come to see me but who really sees me? Most persons only look to the external appearance. It is a pity that few are able to go beyond and penetrate to see the inner Reality. So many people come to see me but few really see me. They go back as they came. So you see my simplicity is really a deception, and today I am revealing it to you!"

Master's impersonal love for his devotees is not shown in grand deeds, but the love is hidden behind every small, insignificant and often unnoticed act in the humble routine of day-to-day existence.

On one of my visits to Shahjahanpur about twenty of us were gathered around him in the open courtyard, Master in a deep canvas deck-chair, the others clustered around him, some on chairs, the others on charpoys or rope-cots. It was after dinner of a late summer evening, not cold but extremely balmy and pleasant. From 9 o'clock the number of persons around Master steadily declined as abhyasis went off to bed, one by one. All slept out in the open on the charpoys. By 11 p.m. there were only three of us with Master, the others by now soundly asleep all around us. Master was answering our questions and revealing many profound things to us, when suddenly and abruptly he arose, went into his room and came back with a blanket in his hands. He walked to the charpoy of an abhyasi sleeping farthest from us, draped the blanket over him, tucked it in under his feet, and then quietly came back to his seat to resume the interrupted conversation. I surmised that the abhyasi must have been feeling cold (he was, I discovered next morning, one of my young colleagues from South India) and somehow Master had divined this, and lovingly covered him with a blanket. Otherwise why should that particular person, and he only, have been singled out for this special attention? No one was more surprised than the abhyasi himself when he woke up next morning to find himself with a blanket over him.

On the three days during which Vasant Panchami is celebrated there is generally a large gathering, with people sleeping around in all the rooms and covered areas. The surplus is accommodated in other buildings nearby. The days are full of activity, and they are long days too as we get up at 4 a.m., and go to bed around midnight. Irrespective of where the abhyasis stay, meals are arranged at Master's residence. Because of the large number present they are fed in batches, and the total service lasts several hours. One evening, on the first occasion when I attended the Vasant Panchami celebrations, I was feeling a bit tired and out of sorts. The first batch for dinner was nearly through but there were so many waiting that I decided to go without dinner, and went to bed. At about 10:30 p.m. I suddenly found Master coming into my room where I had so far been alone. He called me by name and said, "You have not eaten yet. Please come with me. I have prepared a special place for you inside where you can eat. Food has been placed ready for you." I did not know what to say but quietly accompanied him inside. He sat with me while I ate. The significant thing is he did not ask me whether I had eaten or not. He told me that I had not eaten yet and took me inside. People were too busy to have noticed me, but yet Master, with all his preoccupations, had not been too busy to divine that one under his roof had not had his dinner! It was a matter of wonder to me how he had singled me out as perhaps the only person who had not had his dinner. Such episodes, which I have wonderingly seen repeated again and again, have confirmed me in my opinion that Master *feels* within himself everything that all those around him feel — and responds whenever response is necessary. The response may be a physical act as in the episodes related above, or may be a transmission of his own spiritual essence. Master's empathy with others is complete and natural, so natural in fact that he may be said to be a mirror which reflects what is in its presence.

The Vasant Panchami celebrations are held in winter, and winter in Shahjahanpur can be, and generally is, very cold. It is cold enough not only to astonish European visitors but, on occasion, to cause them considerable discomfort too. South Indians unfamiliar with the North generally do not appreciate the severity of the cold, and it is therefore quite normal for one who is on his first winter visit to come totally unprepared to face the climate. Master keeps a small reserve stock of blankets for such visitors. Some of our sisters also knit woolen pull-overs all the year round to keep a small reserve supply available at Mission headquarters in Shahjahanpur. Yet the demand often exceeds the supply. On one occasion Master was seated in his usual corner in the sunny part of the courtyard, his usual winter station. We were a small group around him, on this the day prior to Vasant Panchami day itself. It was about 11 o'clock in the morning, but even out in the sun it was quite cold as the winter that year was rather severe. Master was dressed in his usual fashion in a dhoti and kurta, acknowledging the fact that it was winter by adding a sleeveless woolen pull-over, quite inadequate for that cold, to his attire. He had a blanket covering his knees. His main weapon against the cold seemed to be his hookah, which he was smoking with great relish and visible satisfaction. At this time a South Indian abhyasi walked into the compound, carrying his sole piece of baggage, a hold-all. He was wearing just cotton trousers and a terylene shirt, and was shivering in the cold. He came up to Master and greeted him in the traditional fashion and sat down with us. Master said nothing. He took off his pull-over and asked the abhyasi to wear it. The abhyasi accepted it gratefully. Immediately all of us expostulated with Master, each one of us offering his own pull-over. Master refused our offer, and sat down with a quiet child-like smile on his face. I, for one, felt ashamed that none of us had been able to think of a brother abhyasi's distress, but consoled myself with the thought that Master is unique, and none can be like him in his quick perception of the needs of others, and his immediate and active response to that perception. I have seen this same small but significant drama played over and over again, but to me it comes as a new revelation every time, and the wonder of Master's love never fades by repetition. It is a pity that a silent witness to this drama is often more touched by it than the recipient himself, who often prefers to take away the pull-over as a souvenir.

On another occasion, again at Shahjahanpur, I was lying in bed, tired out and with an ache in the lower limbs. I was alone in the room. Master came in unan-

nounced and I quickly sat up to greet him. He asked me
what was wrong and I told him about the pain in my legs.
He immediately sat down to massage them. I fiercely
remonstrated with him and prevented it. Master said,
"Why do you feel it is wrong? Have you not massaged
my legs and feet so many times? Now when you are in
pain it is my duty to serve you to the best of my ability." I
told Master that as a disciple of his I could not allow him
to massage my legs. Master laughed in a rarely beautiful way. His eyes which are ever dry, even they became
a little moist. He was lost in reminiscence for a moment. Then he said, "Look, I will tell you one thing.
Once I had bad pain in my legs. I was lying alone in bed.
Suddenly I heard Lalaji Saheb asking me why I was in
bed. At that time Lalaji Saheb was already in the
Brighter World. I answered him that I was suffering
from pain in my legs. He offered to massage them but I
remonstrated with him, and Lalaji became silent. Yet a
few seconds later I felt a wonderful vibration in my legs.
Look here! What my Master was doing for me. He was
actually massaging my legs for me. Where can you boys
get a Master like him? My pain left immediately." And
strange to say, as Master concluded this revealing
episode of Lalaji's sacred love for my own Master, my
leg pain seemed to vanish too.

On yet another occasion I was a witness to what has
been, to me, one of the most moving experiences of my
life. The experience of those few moments left me
shaken, moved to the very foundations of my being, and
in tears. It was just after dusk on a long summer day at
Shahjahanpur. A senior preceptor from the South had
come on a visit. Master asked him to have dinner, but
he declined, saying that he generally ate only one meal a
day. He offered to have a glass of milk instead. Master

asked one of the younger abhyasis to fetch two glasses of milk, one for this gentleman and one for my father. The glasses of milk arrived after a few minutes, and these two walked away with them, deep in some discussion between themselves. I was left alone with Master. I asked Master whether I could fetch him a glass of milk too. Master smiled infinitely sweetly and, with a look that had profound compassion in it, answered, "I cannot afford to drink milk." I was shaken to the core by this simple, loving utterance. I did not know what to say or do, but merely sat there in his benevolent presence with tears streaming down my face. This secret drama of Divine hospitality has become such a cherished memory, and so much a part of what I know of my Master, that even now, as I write this, I am profoundly moved by that memory. Alas! How weak and puny we are who, seeing all, are unable to emulate Him in even the least of his gestures.

These, and similar unnoticed dramas have sown the seeds of love for the Master in many many hearts now scattered all over the world. Every new expression of Master's Divine love strengthens us in our love for him. This is the secret of Master's magnetic hold on all those who come into contact with him. Time and again I have seen strangers come into his presence who, when they leave after even a brief chat with him, leave as lovers of the Master. Many have confided that even after a few minutes with Master they have felt as if they have known him all their lives. My Master's spiritual aid is his invincible love in its purest, holiest form — and what is there that can stand up to it and be unconquered? Others may use power, fear, or temptation as instruments to bind their disciples to themselves. My Master's sole instrument is his Divine love for all mankind which demands nothing in return — or if he at all asks for anything it is nothing but our hearts.

I remember one occasion when Master was visiting one of our Mission centres in South India. The gentleman at whose residence we were staying had arranged a grand lunch for about 150 persons. Master ate a few small morsels of the food offered to him, and then sat apart in another room. I quickly finished my lunch and went and sat with him. A little later our host came to Master and asked, "Master, have you had your lunch? Was it satisfactory?" Master smiled and said everything was good, though he could eat but just a little. The host then asked, "Master, is there anything else I can offer you?" Master quietly smiled and answered, "Yes, you can offer me your heart!" Our host obviously took this for a witty remark, for he laughed and walked away to attend to his guests.

I think that because Master's love is so pure and holy, his devotees are able to love him for himself alone. Master's love is so pure and undemanding that abhyasis are able to develop a reciprocal love, purer and undemanding in progressively increasing degrees. As this love develops in the abhyasi, a stage comes when the idea of 'transactions' ceases. There is no more the question of love for, or with, an aim. Love is there because one can no longer live without that love for the Master in the heart. It is a strangely surprising and beautiful thing, but at this stage the idea of being loved by the Master seems to lose its importance. What becomes all-important is the love in one's own heart for the Master. As this love grows and grows a stage comes when it seems as if the heart would verily explode. I consider the growth of this Divine Love to be the greatest miracle in the spiritual development of a person. There is no longer even the faintest thought of what Master can give. Even the Divine gift of liberation, which Master can bestow by a mere glance, loses its importance. All that the aspirant yearns for is to be with his Master, his true beloved. As we bestow our love, Master bestows his love on us, and **this** is Grace, **this** is Liberation, and **this** is the total realisation of the aim of spiritual *sadhana*. Love itself becomes everything, a potent universe-embracing power, which endows by its very presence consciousness of the highest level, call it Divine, call it Cosmic, call it what you will. This love carries within it the quality of divine perception, which Master mundanely calls "reading capacity." Even at the ordinary human level we find love opens closed eyes. One who loves sees more than one who does not. Is it then any wonder that Master with his all-loving vision sees all? Is it any wonder that he sees the hunger of the hungry, the pain of the one in pain, and the craving for spiritual realisation hidden deep in the heart of a devoted aspirant? So, love is a great force which can give us the capacity to 'read', and it is therefore quite understandable that persons who use mere intellectual force or power fail to develop this vision in themselves. We must turn to the heart for this divine faculty. Master repeatedly emphasises the need to turn to the heart. In fact he distrusts the intellect. He has often told me, "The intellect will not provide you with what you want. Its answers are based on the information you provide it. So decisions of the intellect can be wrong, and even immoral. But if you question the heart you will get the correct judgment. When in doubt refer to the heart. It will give you correct guidance."

I once asked Master to reveal to me the secret of quick progress in spirituality. Master said, "Create love in yourself, and then see the progress. Really speaking, love can conquer all, and love alone can do this. Everything else, every other force or power, creates a reaction which is not favourable. If you are annoyed you transmit anger, and the other person becomes angry in turn. If you use physical force, that too creates resistance followed by a reaction on its own plane. It is the same with everything else. But if you create love in your heart, then the reaction is also of love and love alone — and see, your job is done! So create love. It is with love that our ancient *rishis* were able to live in jungles with wild animals all around them. Love conquers even the wild animals. I am telling you one thing. If there is love in your heart for the Master, then the Master begins to love you. If you can bring this about then your work is almost done. The important thing is to knock on the door of his heart so vigorously that he is compelled to open it to you. Then what to say of progress, everything is there for you. What is the abhyasi's real duty? In my opinion he must do everything to make the Master turn towards him — and once that is done the abhyasi can sit back and let the Master work for him. Who can resist love? As the abhyasi's love grows, so also the Master's love grows. And the Master now begins to think what he can do for the abhyasi. It is no longer necessary for the abhyasi to ask. What is there to ask for when the giver is himself thinking about what to give and when? Really speaking, a true Master is nothing but a mirror. What the abhyasi places before it is reflected by it. You understand this? In the Master himself there is nothing. You only take from him what you yourself put into him. Now, I am telling you something. There are people who accuse the guru of being partial to one or another of the abhyasis. Do you see how wrong this idea is? And it is also dangerous, for the idea of distrust and hatred may grow, and these also will be reflected. So we must create love and then see its working. I say it is the most potent power of Divinity."

In my own experience I have known this love of Master for the abhyasi working miracles. Master's love has brought about transformations in the character of abhyasis which no threat or use of power could have brought about. When we are afraid of our Master we do not really change or permit transformation in ourselves. All that we do is to hide certain sides of our life from him, and thus develop a guilt complex on top of the rest. As this trend goes on unchecked the fear of Master increases until a stage must surely come when we cannot even face him. At this stage the idea of separateness comes into play. And as this separateness grows we can almost see the shores of spirituality going below the horizon, as if from a ship leaving port. I once had occasion to write to Master with a sense of guilt in me for something I had done. I wrote to him that I was afraid of even coming into his presence. Master's reply was very prompt. He wrote, "Human beings commit mistakes. I myself commit many mistakes. We must try to rectify ourselves and try to avoid them in the future. Put away this idea of fear. If you allow it to grow it will interfere with your expansion." The advice was very clear and precise. I removed the fear from my heart, as if removing a physical object, and have been free of guilt since then.

How does his love work to transform us? When we know that Master loves us, we begin to feel we must deserve that love. This is the first step in self-evaluation which automatically creates co-operation in the abhyasis. We go on and on, on the spiritual path. To be tempted, or to have to face temptation, is common to all of us. But one who is loved by the Master is immensely superior in his equipment to face trials. At every turn of life when temptations pose a sore trial we ask ourselves, "Would Master approve of this if I did it? What would he feel if I should succumb and fall? Would I not be the cause of much sorrow and disappointment to him if I fail him now after he has bestowed so much labour and love on my spiritual development?" Such questions addressed to ourselves put the matter in clear perspective and, even in the very process of asking them, the temptation is gone. When we realise this, that the trying situation no more challenges us but seems to have disappeared almost like a mirage, then gratitude wells up in the heart for the Grace that averted possible disaster. This in turn strengthens the love in the heart, and so it goes on, every temptation no longer a danger to us, but merely an instrument for strengthening our love for the Master, and making it more and more part of our very essence. Thus love achieves what fear never can, and never will, achieve. Love does not merely strengthen us, but transforms us into vessels containing Divine love, as it were.

Love for the Master makes us long to emulate him, and to grow into a Person like him. This desire to emulate him and be like him is itself a big leap forward on the spiritual path, as it presents to us, for perhaps the first time a clear and well defined goal at which to aim. Hitherto we have had abstract goals like 'perfection' or 'liberation' or the achieving of peace etc. Now the inner aspiration becomes concretised in a definite longing to **be** like something, to **be** like some one. The difference between our earlier, undefined longing and this new, concrete aspiration is an enormous one, because it exhibits a definite change in the mental attitude from one of 'having' to one of 'becoming' and 'being'. As Master pithily puts it, "Prayer is begging," and as long as the idea of 'having' or 'getting' remains in our minds we are nothing but beggars. But now the change that love creates is subtle and definite. When the desire to **be** like Master dawns in our hearts, then we cease to be beggars. We are no longer 'asking' for something, we are **trying to be** something, and so co-operation intensifies, bringing our goal within our grasp.

Soon after Master granted me permission to work as a preceptor I had a short discussion with him on how to do the work of transmission, cleaning etc. He told me a few things and outlined a few techniques to be followed. In conclusion he added, "Think that I am sitting in your place. If necessary imagine that there is a beard on your face and that you are like me. This will help you in the work." At that time I did not understand the importance of this advice sufficiently, but I have always adopted this technique, often to the exclusion of all other techniques, and found the work more rewarding. I have found that the more I am able to imagine I am like the Master, the better the results are for the abhyasi. On certain days 'I' am totally absent and only Master is there. On such days the abhyasi receiving transmission has the greatest benefit, and reports having the best and most tranquil sessions.

Once Master told me a small episode from his own life touching this aspect of spiritual life. Master had prepared himself for his bath and was going to the well to draw water. On the way a tremendous longing flooded his heart — a longing to be like his Master, Lalaji Saheb. As this longing welled up in his heart he heard Lalaji's voice saying, "When this thought has

entered into you, you have already become like me.
Now nothing is wanting."

Master has told me of the love that one of the disciples of Lalaji had for Lalaji Saheb. Master told me
that it was love of the highest order. "Look here, that
sort of love I have rarely seen. You know, he was so attentive to Lalaji that even Lalaji used to be astonished
by it. Once Lalaji was attending his office in the Court.
It was mid-day, and Lalaji had a sudden desire for a cup
of coffee. Now you know that in these parts coffee
drinking is even now very rare. It must have been even
rarer in those days. But within a short time of this desire
coming up, Lalaji saw this disciple coming into court to
see him. He had brought Lalaji some coffee to drink.
Lalaji was greatly pleased by this sign of personal devotion." Master continued, "Now look here, how attentive
he was to his Master's needs. I will tell you a more
wonderful thing. Lalaji used to get up sometimes at
night to go to the bathroom. But do you know, he would
invariably find that particular abhyasi ready with a pot
of water and a towel for Lalaji's wash. You understand
what this means? Even in his sleep the abhyasi had
been receptive and alert to his Master's needs. That is
why he was able to get up even before Lalaji himself
woke up, and to be ready for him. That is love of the
highest quality." Impulsively, on the spur of the moment, I asked Master how it transpired that that
particular abhyasi did not become Lalaji's Spiritual
Representative and Successor. I could have bitten my
tongue off, but there it was, the question had been
asked, and I expected the worst for my gross imper-
tinence. But Master smiled and answered, "You know,
every moth can immolate itself in a living flame, but
rare is the moth that can immolate itself in a cold

flame." Once again I was too deeply moved to say anything more. What did this statement of Master's mean?
What was its spiritual import? The answer, hidden behind the words, was clear. Human love, even of a very
high order, dies when the object of its love is no longer
present before it. Divine love exists for ever unto all
eternity. It is a love which has penetrated into the most
secret and mysterious depths of the Master's being and
found Him to be eternally present. Such a love knows
no death, acknowledges no absence, experiences no
separation.

Part II

His Teaching and Work

"I saw Eternity the other night,
Like a great Ring of pure and endless Light,
All calm as it was bright;
One whispered thus:
"This Ring the Bridegroom did for none provide
But for His Bride."

Vaughan The Silurist

VI

The Way of the Spirit

From time immemorial the religious life has been held up as the summit of human existence. This has been so in all the nations of the world, primitive and advanced. Religious activity has ever been described as the highest type of human activity, and the religious life *per se* extolled as the perfect culmination to all human endeavour. There has always been a special halo around the initiated aspirant, and naturally the ordained priests enjoyed a far higher special status of their own. The power and prestige of the priesthood or clergy was often of such magnitude as to eclipse that of the temporal rulers of the times. India has had more than its fair share of religions, having given birth to two of the world's great systems, Hinduism and Buddhism. India has also been one of those countries where religion has permeated into practically every sphere of human existence. The Hindu religion takes hold of the individual soon after his conception, and releases him only after he is dead, his body cremated, and his ashes ceremoniously offered into the water of a river or the sea. Every aspect of the individual's life in-between these two extreme situations is governed by rituals appropriate to the occasion.

The great seers of India, the rishis, have bifurcated the holy life into two distinct approaches to Reality, the ritualistic life, and the contemplative life. The texts of Hinduism are correspondingly categorised, and the *Vedas* themselves come under this categorisation. The earlier parts, dealing almost exclusively with rituals, are classified under the term *karma kanda*. The later portions of the *Vedic* text, the *Gnana Kanda*, deal mostly with the mental and higher aspects of man's approach to his Maker, and are commonly called *Vedanta*, translated to mean "the end of all knowledge." *Vedanta* does not merely mean that this part of the *Vedic* teaching comes at the serial end of the *Veda*. It means that here is contained such knowledge as can be considered to be the end of all knowledge, the very acme and essence of knowledge.

The rishis have also taught, very clearly and emphatically, that the ritualistic religious life is a lower aspect of man's existence, whereas the contemplative life is extolled as being the higher and purer one. The texts themselves are explicit in their statement that formal rules and restrictions apply only to the ritual performances, where strict prescriptions as to place, time and method of performance are to be implicitly followed. In the contemplative life such restrictions no longer bind a person. He has escaped out of the physical rigidity of ritual religious performance into the freedom of mental contemplation of the Divine.

With such a clear enunciation of principles of worship one would have expected to find the people able to follow them without difficulty. But it is mystifying to find that something akin to almost utter confusion prevails. The average person seems to prefer to stick to the bondage of the ritual life. It has this attraction that so long as one obeys the priestly injunctions for a stated period of time — generally curtailed to a few minutes a day — he enjoys a liberty that is almost permissive the rest of the time. In the contemplative life, or the life of the mystic, there is a freedom that does not exist at

lower levels of existence, but this freedom appears un-
attractive to most persons, as it carries within itself the
need for responsible action by the person. Such a person has to prescribe for himself the ethical and moral
values that guide his life. No longer can he merely obey
a set of rules often elastically interpreted by his priestly
guide. Now the onus of leading a right life is on him,
and on him alone. So the apparent freedom of the
spiritual life seems to have hidden within it the greater
bondage of self-discipline, self-control and so on, culminating in the principle of self-surrender. When this is
understood, people seem to prefer the total lack of
freedom during a specified period under the ritual life
to the apparent freedom of the contemplative.

There was once an interesting discussion on this
subject of freedom. An overseas preceptor had been
listening to Master talking about the freedom that a
spiritual life offered. Master had been talking about
this for some time. When Master stopped, this
gentleman asked, "But Master, to me it appears that the
freedom is becoming less and less as we progress. You
ask us to surrender to Master. Is it not then a total loss
of freedom?" Master answered, "Yes, you are right. But
I take charge of you only to finally hand you over to
God. This can be done only under such conditions."
The gentleman then asked, "But then the freedom does
not exist as you say. What is the real freedom, Master?"
Master answered, with a serious expression on his face,
"Really speaking the only freedom is the freedom to do
the right. There is no other freedom." I have brooded
over this off and on over the years, and I have come to
the conclusion that this is indeed the only freedom.

A motor car on the street has freedom, but only to
go where it is permitted. It may not enter a one-way

street from the wrong end; it may not exceed speed limits specified; it may park only in areas specifically set aside for this purpose, and so on. Within the framework of these regulations the driver enjoys complete freedom. Why are these rules, restrictive rules, made? They are for the safety of the driver himself. If there was only one car in a city the rules need not be so rigid. When there are more, then laws get progressively more in number, and more and more restrictive too. While on its rails a train is free. If it leaves the rails there is disaster. We think an aeroplane pilot to be a 'free' person, and we have, most of us, at one time or the other, been envious of the total freedom that the pilot apparently enjoys. We look on enviously, and wish we were up there in the sky, free to do as we please. But alas! this freedom too is illusory. The pilot is strictly controlled in virtually everything he does. His take-off time is controlled; his route is strictly charted and laid down; his speed is controlled; also his altitude and so on. But within these limits he is free to do as he wishes. An aeroplane pilot has considerably **less** freedom than a car driver on the road has. When we see the working of the astronauts we discover, to our dismay, that the freedom of action has almost completely disappeared. Their every action is rigidly controlled. Not merely are the mechanical details such as the times of flight, route, etc., all rigidly laid down but even personal routines such as their sleep and rest periods, what to eat and when, are clearly stipulated. It is a matter of wonder that these persons have been able to so completely subject themselves to this rigid discipline and that they are able to perform as required. The reason is very clear. If they did not, they would cease to exist. The penalty for disobedience is the awful one of death, instantaneous

death. At this level obedience of the total variety is
what is imperatively necessary, as it decides whether a
person will continue to exist or not! We thus see that
freedom appears to carry the seeds of potential disaster
within itself.

It seems clear that at lower levels of activity the apparent freedom of the individual is greater, while the
activity itself seems to need a lesser degree of ability for
its performance. As the plane of activity rises, the
ability needed for its right performance is more and
more, while individual freedom appears to become less
and less, and simultaneously the need for stricter
obedience increases stage by stage. At the highest
levels the individual's freedom seems to be virtually
non-existent, to have vanished! The need for obedience
is now total; and the ability needed for the correct performance of one's duty is of the level of the *adept*. We
appear to have arrived at the stage where the only
freedom is indeed the freedom to do what is right! But,
and this appears to me a significant point, the entire
training to bring a person to the level of the adept
seems, finally, to culminate in making that person
instinctively and completely obedient to Master's orders. When a person has progressed to this level there
is no thinking, no reasoning. When an order is given by
the Master the necessary activity issues forth, almost at
the level of a reflex action. This, I feel, is what distin-
guishes a real adept from a merely capable person who
has not developed this ability for perfect, unthinking
and instantaneous obedience.

Here we find a law working — as we rise higher and
higher our freedom becomes less and less! At least this
is apparently what happens. But is this really so? It all
depends on our ideas of freedom, the ways in which we

have been trained to think about it. After having examined this concept of freedom in quite some detail
over many years of puzzled thought, I have come to the
conclusion that the ideas I have held all these years are
almost entirely wrong. The whole idea of freedom
seems, to me, to be illusory. Or rather, to put it in
another way, the lower levels of existence, of uncom-
mitted existence, seem to enjoy some degree of
freedom; but this progressively shrinks until, at the
highest level, there is no freedom at all. But, and here
lies the difference, **there is no bondage either!** The mistake, I believe, lies in identifying a state of non-freedom
with a state of bondage. They are not identical by any
means. This is the same mistake we make when we
think of a person without wealth as a poor person, or of
a person without knowledge as an ignorant person.
What we have to perceive is that there is an in-between
state in every case, a sort of zero point, which is a totally
unconditioned state, and this I believe to be the true
state of spiritual existence.

To consider this a little further, suppose a person
wishes to tell a lie, say about his age. He has considerable freedom in choosing a figure to mention as his
age, but to tell the truth there is no freedom whatsoever
since the correct figure can be one, and one only.
Similarly the shortest distance between two points can
only be one, but many longer ways can exist, and these
can be as many as we care to choose. We thus see that to
tell a lie, or to follow a wrong path, many ways exist.
That is, there is apparently a great degree of freedom.
Whereas for right conduct, right speech no freedom exists as there is only one way and we have to follow it. As
a person evolves spiritually, and progresses to higher
and yet higher levels of existence, the whole universe of

unlimited choice that he had at the beginning has now become narrowed down to just one goal, with but one path to lead up to it. To tread such a path no skill or ability is required, perhaps no knowledge even is necessary. All that is now necessary is an unquestioning obedience of the Master's instructions. This alone will ensure successful, safe and early completion of the spiritual quest.

This also helps us to see why, in Sahaj Marg, no qualifications are considered necessary in an aspirant. The sole qualification, as I have elaborated elsewhere, is that of willingness to follow the Master obediently.

In examining this idea of freedom we have been led to the conclusion that what we have thought of as loss of freedom is really nothing but a state of surrender to the Master's will. We have not lost freedom in the sense that we have been deprived of it. We have voluntarily, whole-heartedly and devotedly surrendered it to the Master of our Soul. We now see why the need for such surrender is paramount. Choice implies knowledge of how to choose, and will to enforce that choice. Our choice was exercised when we chose the Master and his way. It is like a bachelor who has virtually unlimited choice of a bride, but having chosen one and married her, the question of further choice no longer arises! The time for choice is over. At higher and higher levels of evolution the very idea of choice ceases to exist. A stage has now been reached where even knowledge is no longer necessary. Many great saints have testified from their personal spiritual experience that a stage is reached when we have to bid knowledge and the intellect good-bye. It is not that we abandon knowledge as being unworthy or incapable of helping us. It served its role, its part has been played out, and the time for it to leave the stage has come, that is all! All that we need now is will, will to act and will to obey the Master in every single instruction. To those who are fortunate enough to arrive at this exalted stage the Master is no longer a guide for spirituality alone. He has now become the Master of one's life in all its aspects of existence. He becomes the father, the mother, the son, the teacher, the doctor, in fact there is no role that He does not play in the abhyasi's life! He has taken total charge of the abhyasi. So we see that only our surrendering to him can bring about a state where he can take total charge of us!

Analysing this further we find, surprisingly, that a great and unimaginable freedom is now conferred on the abhyasi. **It is the freedom from freedom itself!** It is the freedom of invulnerability. We may even say that it is the freedom of invincibility. We are no longer answerable for our actions. We merely obey. The person who issues the orders, the Master, assumes complete responsibility for everything we do. We are no longer vulnerable to the world. Therefore a great calm, a great freedom comes to us. Out of an apparent loss of a previous freedom, largely illusory as we have seen, we now receive as a Divine gift the true freedom of a spiritual state, a real freedom which some saints have called the "Great Liberation".

We thus see that where religion binds, spirituality liberates. The great seers and mystics of all religions have taught this, but few have followed them. Many read and hear but few understand. Of those who understand few are bold enough to shake off the chains of traditional bondage and undertake the quest anew. To these few comes the realisation that they have sought, and when it comes they wonder at the splendour and magnificence of the truth they have been seeking, which its own utter simplicity and proximity have kept hidden from us.

I have discussed the role of traditional forms of worship again and again with my Master. On one occasion I requested Master to elaborate on the drawbacks, if any, of traditional methods of worship. I asked Babuji, "Master, these ways have been followed for so many thousands of years. How can they be unsatisfactory? Have they not been responsible for our rishis and saints achieving the goal of unity with the Divine? I am unable to follow this. Kindly explain a little more in detail." Master answered, "I am not saying the traditional ways are bad or wrong. All that I say is that the method of approach must be correct according to your goal, and if your goal is Realisation then the way must be subtle and correctly followed. So the person, whoever it is, must first determine his goal, and only then arises the question of the way of achieving it. But the individual person has to decide the goal for himself. Nobody else can do this for him. Now suppose you have as your goal the earning of large wealth. You will first look for the person who can help you to earn it. If you want to develop a strong body you will go to a *pahalwan* or physical culturist. So the goal first, then the guide. The trouble is we see many many persons around us who have attached themselves to one guru or another without knowing why. How many of these persons know what they are looking for? Is it then any wonder that they do not know what they are doing, and why? This is the difficulty, that we blindly do what others have done. I am telling you one thing. Discrimination is necessary. We must be able to decide for ourselves as to what is good for us. Confusion must be thrown aside. Then the goal can be easily reached. But I tell you, people find it difficult to change their ways. Change is always difficult if people have no discrimination or will to change. But as I have told you there can be no progress without change. People follow a certain way of rituals or worship. Everybody sees, and says, 'Look! What a pious person this is. He is holy!' and so on. This gives great satisfaction. The ego is satisfied. Does such a person really want God or Realisation? Think it over! So you see, **why** we do something is as important as **how** we do it. You see the basic approach is itself not correct. How can there be success?"

"Master! What about those who are sincere and serious in their search?" I asked. Master said, "Yes, for them the goal is established as a real goal. Now we come to the *marg* or way. I have already told you that God is simple and the way of attaining Him must likewise be simple. I have written in *Reality at Dawn* that to pick up a needle we would not use a crane! My associates appreciate this very much. Have you read Kabir? He has written that if the water of the Ganga is holy then every crocodile in it should get *moksha*! You see this? A gross act cannot lead to a subtle result. We must try to understand this. We have become lost in our ritualistic way of life. It is generally easy to follow, and gives much satisfaction of having done our duty. But what we don't realise is that it is adding grossness to us. I will tell you of a case which came to me. A person had been doing puja for many years. He used to imagine that God was seated in his heart, and that he was doing *pradakshina* or circumambulation round him hundred times or thousand times, I don't remember. One day he came to me. Maybe Dr. Varadachari brought him to me. I don't recollect. I examined his condition. You know what I found? His heart was all wrapped up like a silk-worm in a cocoon! The heart was under great strain, which he did not feel. At first I did not understand how this had happened, but when he told me the method of worship he had been adopting then I understood. See what havoc it had done. Poor man, he thought he had been doing a very pious thing, but really he had put himself in serious difficulties. Do you remember the other experience I told you? The one about the monkey!" (with much laughter). I recalled what Master was referring to. Master had personally conducted satsangh at one of our South Indian centres. About forty or fifty persons were present and the sitting lasted about twenty- five minutes. Later, when we were alone, Master told me that soon after he commenced transmission he got the impression that a monkey was sitting in the group. He opened his eyes and found an abhyasi of long association sitting there. He closed his eyes and in a few moments the same experience was repeated — the monkey was again there! Master once again opened his eyes and found the abhyasi there. Master said, "You know, I could hardly control my laughter. When I opened my eyes this abhyasi was there, when I closed them a monkey was there. Do you know the reason? I will tell you. I examined the case and found that he had been doing Hanuman worship for a very long time, maybe in some past life, and the impressions were there, very strong and deeply buried. During cleaning the impressions must have come to the surface of the mind. Therefore I had the impression of a monkey sitting there!"

Master has given many similar examples of grossness arising out of wrong approaches to worship. In some cases the grossness is deeply embedded, and so hard, that virtually no help can be given. I asked Master how this could happen, that he himself was unable to help. Master replied, "I will tell you. I have had some cases where the heart is surrounded by grossness so hard that it is like a rock. It appears as if the heart is embedded in solid rock. If you give transmission in such cases it will just come back to you." I asked Master whether, in such cases, nothing could at all be done. Was there no way out for them? Master answered, "Well, if the power is used it can be done. There is no doubt about it. But the danger is there that in breaking the grossness the person himself may be affected. The process will have to be very slow, and only complete co-operation on the part of the abhyasi can help him. In such cases I suggest that they pray sincerely to God daily for help. Later on the case can be taken up for deep cleaning." I related to Master a somewhat graphic experience I had had once with an abhyasi. I was carrying out the process of cleaning when, suddenly, a vision came before my eyes, and I saw a giant sewer, bigger than a man, pouring out sewage of such a filthy condition that I was momentarily nauseated. Master said, "Yes, that is the work of the preceptor. I told you a Master is nothing but a sweeper. But the whole problem is only when working in the heart region. Really speaking the heart region is the gutter of humanity. We have to dive into this and do the work. Yes, once the abhyasi progresses and rises to the mind region, then the work becomes a pleasure. After that not much effort is needed. A capable Master can do the work by a mere glance. Now I am telling you one thing. In my own interest I move people quickly out of the heart region. After all who would like to work there longer than necessary? But co-operation of the abhyasi can speed up the process, and save me a great deal of trouble and work."

Master narrated to me another experience relating to cleaning. On that occasion he had gone to Benares, and unwittingly had strayed into a street with an unsavoury reputation. He instinctively felt that he was in the wrong place. At that moment he heard Lalaji's voice asking, "What are you doing in this place?" Master was nonplussed, and answered, "Saheb, I am here by mistake. I do not know where I am." Lalaji said, "Since you are here, let the people of this place derive some benefit from your presence. Clean the atmosphere of this locality as you go." Master laughed and added, "I obeyed Lalaji's orders. Now look at His greatness. He did not chide me for going there. But his love for humanity is seen in his order to me. We must always strive that wherever we may go, we must leave the light of Reality burning there. Lalaji Saheb was transmitting continuously all the twenty-four hours of the day. Even when travelling he would continue to transmit. Where can we get such a Master? Really speaking Lalaji is a prodigy of nature!"

Hearing this mention of Lalaji's name, I was curious to know from my Master whether Lalaji had himself practised any ritual forms of puja. Master fell into a ruminative mood. He said, "I will tell you one thing. Lalaji Saheb had the greatest respect for tradition. He would never criticise anything or anybody. He taught people what he knew was the best approach to one's goal, but he always did this without decrying other systems of puja or worship. That is why he was a very popular person, and people of all castes and communities used to go to him for advice and guidance. They had faith in him because he always gave the correct guidance in all matters. But I tell you one thing, he was much against rituals. He had a very pious and religious mother, but she passed away when Lalaji was very young. In her time he used to sing for her. Lalaji had a most beautiful voice which all loved to hear. He used to sing devotional songs, and one of his favourite songs was *Dinana dukh haran Nath santana hitkari*. It is a great pity that in his days there were no tape records or such things. Yes, he never did ritual worship. But I will tell you one thing. One *Amavasya* day (new moon day) I saw him performing the *tarpana*. He was pouring water in the ritual fashion, offering it to his forefathers in the higher world. I immediately adjusted myself to see what he was really doing. It was wonderful to observe it. I found that he was transmitting the essence of the water he was offering to the higher world. Do you understand this? This is what should be done when offering *bhog*. Now I am telling you something. Suppose a person can transmit the essence of a thing, then it is useful to do *tarpana* and all these things. Otherwise what is the use? It is a mere ritual without any meaning or use. It is better to sit in meditation and think of the departed souls. Surely they will benefit more by it. And if a person is a preceptor he should transmit with the idea that the transmission will reach the soul wherever it may be. You see, the ways of helping are there. But what can we do if the people stick to the gross forms of rituals out of ignorance and fear?"

On one occasion I had a discussion with Master about temple worship. Master had told me that all religions depended on two instruments, and these were fear and temptation. To Master the idea of anyone approaching God out of fear was totally abhorrent. "When we are afraid of something, we run away from it. That is

the natural reaction. Then how can we go towards God
with fear of Him in our hearts! It is not possible. Fear
can only turn us away from Him. I am telling you that
any system which depends on fear will only turn people
away from God. Now you see, to counter-act this they
use the other weapon of temptation — temptation of
material welfare, riches, health, and finally of *moksha*.
Now this temptation works to some extent, but people
only want what they can see or smell — physical things.
So when they seek such *sansthas* they go only for
material benefits. As a result religion has slowly become diluted. The ideals have fallen systematically.
Now people have come to such a low level that they are
prepared to do business with God. You know, I am told
that some businessmen make God a partner in their
business! Is it not something to wonder at? What
foolishness is this? Everything in the universe belongs
to Him and Him alone. What we get, we get from Him.
But people have now begun to think that they have
'earned' what they have. This is ignorance. And they
add to this by arrogantly offering God a share of their
income. Look how foolish and selfish they are. They
think they can bribe God to give them more and more
so that He can get a bigger share for Himself! So you
see all this has to be changed. A person must follow the
right way of Love, and seek God for Himself alone, and
not for what He can give us."

I narrated a short version of a long discussion I once
had with Dr. Varadachari at Tirupathi about temple
worship. Some persons present were of the opinion that
we should not try to wean away persons from their own
traditional practices as it might do harm. Others felt
that temples had been with us for centuries and surely
our ancients knew what they were doing when they built

them, and established them as centres of prayer. Dr.
Varadachari brought a new angle to the whole matter of
temple worship. He explained that few persons were
sufficiently developed to attract a living, personal guru.
It needed a fairly high level of development before an
individual could even think of a guru. What, then, were
they to do? Such persons, who were at lower levels of
development, formed the bulk of humanity. The great
teachers of religion had therefore created the institution of temple worship for this large mass of humanity.
To these people the temple acted as an inanimate guru.
Saints of the past had consecrated these temples and
charged the idols by filling them with power. Such char-
ges were by no means eternal. They would last for a
particular length of time, depending on the power and
development of the saint who had charged the idol.
Once the charge was exhausted the temple could no
longer confer any benefit on persons who prayed there.
Dr. Varadachari added that this was why some temples
fell into disuse and became mere archaeological relics.
He continued to say that the practice of taking a baby
and having its head shorn in the temple was in the nature of an initiatory rite. The child was symbolically
offered to the presiding deity of the temple, and thereafter the child became a disciple of that deity. Dr.
Varadachari then made a very significant statement.
He added that when the child grew up into a man, that
person should seek a living guru suitable to his further
development. And if he was spiritually ready he would
certainly find a guru appropriate to his own level of
development. At this stage temple worship had to be
dropped and the higher spiritual approach taken up for
further development in accordance with the guru's

teaching. This was the gist of Dr. Varadachari's long
talk on this subject.

Master agreed that temple worship had a place in
the general scheme. "But", he asked, "where are the
saints today who have the power of filling power into
idols? If they can do it then there is some meaning in it.
I will tell you another thing. If a person who is capable
of transmission exists, should we receive transmission
from him, or ask him to charge an idol and then pray to
it for development? You understand this idea? We
must go direct, follow the direct way. We should have
no intermediaries between ourselves and God. Of
course if one can find a Master who is himself in *laya*
with God, then he can be taken as a guide. Otherwise it
is no use. It is better to be without a guru than to be with
a wrong person. Without a guru we may not progress,
but with a wrong person we may go backwards and fall.
This is the great danger. Now I tell you one important
thing. Note it carefully. Idol worship is not entirely
wrong. It is wrong only if done in the wrong way. What
is the right way? We should not worship the idol, but
should worship God whom it represents. That is the
correct way. The idol is merely a figure or repre-
sentation of God to remind the devotee and to help him
to bring his mind to a contemplative state. What do we
do? We worship the idol itself as God. This is the great
error, and so grossness grows. Really speaking God has
no form or name. It is we who give these forms and
names to God. By doing this we impose limitations on
Him. Then grossness begins to form. Look at this
foolishness, we should try to expand and grow, but instead of that we are actually trying to limit God
Himself! Can such practices ever lead us to the goal? I
will tell you another important thing. People worship

many gods, but we should worship the God from whom all these gods derive not only their power but their very existence. We should go to the Source. That should be our approach. Anything less than that will make us fall short of the goal and create grossness. I will tell you another thing. People do *tirtha yatra*. They go from place to place and spend many years and a lot of money in bathing in holy rivers and praying at famous temples. Some do this all their lives. But what is the result? Have they derived any spiritual benefit? They only get the satisfaction that they have bathed in so many places and worshiped in so many temples. That is all. I am telling you a very important thing. The real *yatra* is the inner *yatra* of the Soul. That is the true *yatra*. This is what we do in our practice. After all, in the spiritual journey it is not the travel of the body that takes us to the goal (laughing). It is the Soul which has become imprisoned in the heart that has to be made to move; and then to go up point by point until the destination is reached. This is the real *yatra*. I will tell you one more thing", Master went on to say. "There is no mention of temple worship in the *Vedas*. After all, we quote the *Vedas* as our authority for everything that we do. But they say nothing about temples. Dr. Varadachari has confirmed this. You know he has studied the *Vedas* and he is a philosopher. He told me that not only is there no mention of temples in the *Vedas*, really speaking during *Vedic* times temples did not exist at all. Does this mean that people did not pray in those times? What it really means is that temples are not *essential* for prayer. God is everywhere. We must also be able to pray anywhere and this is possible. Everything in nature speaks of the presence of God. Is there anything that does not speak of God's presence? The whole universe is His creation and He is in every atom of it. So prayer must be possible anywhere. The idea of setting apart a separate place for prayer is a much later development, when man grew away from nature. In Vedic times man was part of nature, part of his environment, and saw God in everything. That is why they worshipped rain and thunder and fire and all these things. It is a pity foreigners have misunderstood this, and said that the Hindus worship these material elements. This is not the correct idea. Really speaking the ancients saw God in everything and went into ecstasies, and prayed to everything as Divine. They did not worship fire but worshipped the God that fire represented, and similarly with other things. This is the same idea I told you about idol worship. But later these ideas became debased. Now I want to tell you a good definition of prayer. Our Master Saheb, Mr. Ishwar Sahai, was once asked what prayer is. Master Saheb said it is really an expression of gratitude to God for all that we receive. Now we eat rice and wheat and ghee and so many other things. We are naturally grateful to them. But can we say, 'thank you rice, thank you wheat' and so on? No! So we say thank you to the Creator of all these things, and that is God. So prayer should really be a feeling of gratitude in our heart, not begging for more things. If we ask for more and more it only shows ingratitude for all that we have already received, and I consider it to be the greatest crime against God."

Master continued, "By Lalaji's Grace we have an easy way of achieving our goal. It is the most natural and simple way that he has made available to us. It is really a Sahaj Marg — a simple and natural way of God Realisation. But I am telling you, few persons appreciate its efficacy because they wonder how something so simple and easy can yield such wonderful results! People have become used to following difficult methods, methods requiring long years of strenuous practices. And now when we say God can be easily attained, they are suspicious about it. But if we are wise we must choose the correct way to lead us to our goal, not the most difficult. They prefer to beg for more and more material benefits whereas in our method we **receive** Divine grace from the beginning. I have said prayer is begging but meditation is receiving. Why? Because when we sit for meditation we sit in a receptive attitude so that a vacuum is created in the heart. Only an empty vessel can be filled! Who can fill a vessel that is already full? You see the difference? They beg (laughing), while we receive! This is the greatness of our system. It is Lalaji's grace that such a simple system of greatest efficacy is available to us today. But few take advantage of it. What to say, many people even say they have no time! I prescribed one hour for the morning meditation originally. Now I have reduced it to half-an-hour. Even this people are not willing to do. I will tell you an enjoyable story. A person once came to me. He was a big officer of the government at Delhi. He came to me with one of our associates. he wanted to know something about our system and so I told him. When he heard that he had to meditate for half-an-hour he said it was impossible, as he was too busy to spare so much time. So I asked him to reduce it. He again said he was too busy. I then told him to do 10 minutes a day. Look here! He got angry. He said, 'What is this tamasha! I am telling you I am a very busy man and you are going on asking me to do it. I cannot spare even five minutes a day.' Now Lalaji gave me an idea. Look how he helps us! I asked this officer, 'Can you tell me whether there is anybody more busy than you?' He got angry again. He said, 'What a foolish question this is? Of course there are people more busy than I am. The Prime Minister is much more busy than I am!' I then told him not to take an extreme example but to think of someone just a little more busy than him. He said his neighbour was a bigger officer and more busy than himself. So you know what I told him? (exploding into laughter) I told him, 'Saheb, give me the difference between your busyness and his busyness. That will give some time for meditation.' Poor man, he thought I was making fun of him and he went away quite annoyed."

Master then told me another instance of like nature when a person claimed he was too busy to meditate. Master said, "You know what I told him? I told him God is to be blamed for not creating the day with more than 24 hours in it. It is God's fault. If he had created the day with 26 hours such busy persons would have had time for meditation." Master added, "I have told you, only **he** will get whom He chooses. So what can I do? Anyway we do our work and leave the rest to Master."

Photo by: M. Jean-Marie Bottequin

VII
Approach to Reality

How and when does the search for an undefined goal really commence? In most cases the first faint stirrings of longing seem to be lost in the childhood memories of the individual. Many aspirants testify to this fact that the first spiritual stirrings, the memory of such stirrings, lies in their adolescence, but became buried under later pressures of worldly existence. In a few fortunate cases the reawakening appears to occur, or again once the person had settled down in life. In the majority of cases, however, the reawakening of spiritual desire had to await the onset of middle age, and in many such cases the reawakening appears to occur, or to have occurred, only at periods of personal crisis. In quite a few cases the first stirrings of late childhood lie dormant and latent, to find re-expression in old age. In such cases the chances of success are far less than in other cases unless they are able to attract Master's attention by love and devotion. Master once told me that he had done something really important for an aged abhyasi. He said, "Look here, he is an old man and so out of pity I have given him this as a gift. I did it because he is very devoted and sincere. Old people do not have much time to work, so I give them like this, but you young persons will have to work for your development."

Coming back to the question of the beginning of the search, this depends on the individual, and on the environment and the nature of its pressures on the individual. It is generally accepted that the seed is within the individual as part of his karmic or samskaric heritage. The seed however, has to find the appropriate environmental conditions for its germination. The subsequent conditions have to continue to be favourable for the seedling to grow into a tree of full stature. Such environmental conditions have to be created, first and foremost, in the family or domestic environment. Here in the cradle and by the hearth the seed may germinate, given right conditions. If this early environment is antagonistic to the germination of the karmic impulses to spiritual search, the later struggle, if it happens at all, is liable to be a long and bitter one. A study of the early life of the Grand Master and my Master reveals that they both had serenely pious parents, particularly mothers, with a positive attitude towards the higher life. Their respective family atmospheres were therefore congenial and fostered such development.

I remember my wife Sulochana once asking Master when a person should commence spiritual sadhana. She asked this because Master does not normally permit persons below 18 years of age to meditate. Master answered, "Really speaking the process should begin with conception. Lalaji used to say this, that this was the correct moment for commencing *sadhana*. But how to fix the moment of conception? It is not possible, and so the work cannot be practically commenced then. Therefore what we do is to transmit to the mother while she is carrying, and the transmitted power will automatically reach the baby in correct dosage. One should never transmit direct to the child — this can be highly dangerous. But we should only transmit to the mother, to her heart, as we normally do." Cases where a mother is herself on the path, and thereby is able to confer the divine gift of spiritual training while the growing baby is still part of her, are very rare. But what Master said serves to emphasise the need for the real search to commence as early as possible — the earlier the better.

I had a friend and colleague who was interested in the spiritual life, but in a rather timid and distant manner. I had tried to get him to start meditation. He always kept putting it off saying that he was yet young, unmarried and had plenty of time for "this sort of thing." His objection to commencing spiritual practice was that he had yet to go through the mill of family life, and therefore sadhana of any sort would be premature until he had gone through that particular mill. He got married. I again spoke to him about sadhana, but his reply now was that as he had just been married, he needed some more years to get used to that life. He requested me to wait until he was 50 years old when he would certainly take up spiritual *sadhana*. The tragic part of the matter is that within two years of his marriage he suddenly passed away after a brief and minor illness. It is one of my great regrets that he could not be brought on to the path when the possibility was there.

A second case comes to my mind, more fortunate than the preceding one. This concerns an abhyasi who was, at that time, the only abhyasi from his city. He showed great interest in our system of meditation, and practised the meditation according to my Master's teaching. He was developing so well that Master had him in mind for future work in his city as a preceptor. Unfortunately he suddenly fell ill, and after a very short time he expired. I wrote to Master about him. Master replied that he had examined the matter and that he found the soul of the abhyasi sitting bewildered in a corner. He added, "I have done what was necessary for him. He will be reborn once more, and the next life will be his last." He ended the letter with a most significant sentence. "Had he practised our meditation for even a few months more there would have been the possibility of liberation in this life itself. As it is, one more birth will be necessary." I am referring to these two cases to drive home as strongly as possible the urgent need for **immediate action.** The possibility of liberation is **now,** in the present. Who can say what will happen in the future? 'Never put off till tomorrow what you can do today' is more relevant to spiritual *sadhana* than anything else.

I will record a third case, narrated to me by my Master himself, to show how putting off the quest may delay it indefinitely, perhaps for many lives. Master said, "Look here, persons who come to me are generally at the first point. The *yatra* has not commenced. This is the normal thing. Once a person came to me, and what to say of him, I found him already at the fourth point. It was a high level of attainment and showed his work in his past life. He came to me once, but never returned again. His *samskara* must have prevented it. If he had come back his progress was certain. A little cleaning would have made quick progress possible. It is a pity that he never came back. Now who knows how many lives he may need to find the way! It is the only case which came to me already so highly developed." This shows us the imperative need of achieving our goal in this life itself. We are here. Our Master is available to us, and this life is certain, whatever be its length. Our solemn duty to ourselves is to ensure that with his assistance we complete our journey to our destination within this life — the only one we can be certain of.

As Master himself explained to me on a different occasion, this life is one that we are sure of. We are living it. It needs no proof that it exists. As regards the past life or future lives, different religions teach differently about it. The important thing is that, for our purpose, the whole question of past and future lives becomes irrelevant to the issue of spiritual realisation. We are here living this life; the Master is with us; and the goal exists; a combination of the three factors must enable us to reach our goal in **this** life. This is the importance of Sahaj Marg teaching. I personally may believe in past and future lives. This has been the teaching of the religion into which I have been born. Such a belief may therefore be natural to me. But a similar belief in other persons is unnecessary as far as spiritual practice is concerned. All that concerns us now are the supreme and perceivable truths of our existence, of our Master's existence, and of the existence of a goal to be realised — here and now!

On yet another occasion someone raised the question of many lives being needed to reach the goal. He quoted the *Bhagavad Gita* where Shri Krishna says that even people of great knowledge reach Him only after many lives, Master said, "It may be so. But I am telling you an important thing. It is a sign of weakness to think that the goal is far off and the journey a very difficult one. I say at least start the journey, then you will know what it is really like. Otherwise it is only weakness to go by what others say. You take at least one step in the right direction and see how it is. Then decide. I am telling you another thing. Everybody who comes to me says this thing requires many lives. But why do you assume that this is your first life? Why don't you think this is your last life and therefore in this life itself the goal must be reached? You understand what I am saying? One is a way of weakness, the other is a positive

approach. Who can say with certainty how many lives
we have yet to live. I say it is in our hands to decide it. If
we adopt the right process under the Real Master then
there need be no future lives. So forget this idea of
more lives. We must not look to the next life to continue our journey. Who knows in what environment we
may be born, and how our life is going to be moulded?
It is easy to lose the way. I say, once you find the Master
and the method, stick to them. Bind the Master to yourself in such a way that the bond is a permanent one.
Then success is assured."

Having examined when the search begins, let us see
how it begins. Master has recorded his own personal experiments with ritual performances of religion, and
subsequent yogic practices advocated by hatha yoga followed, finally, by his graduation into the life of spiritual
sadhana. He started his experiments even while he was
a school boy. What we have to note carefully from his
life is that his experiments were conducted sincerely
and meticulously. When the methods proved insuffi-
cient for the realisation of his personal goal he
abandoned them. He did not allow himself to be made
a prisoner of methods which could not help him. The
methods received a sincere and fair trial and, when
found inadequate, were abandoned. He had the great
courage to do this because he knew precisely what he
was looking for. He was not for satisfaction of the ego,
he was not for fulfilling society's dictates; he was not for
name, fame or riches. What he wanted was God and
God alone. So, having tried many approaches, he abandoned them, and resorted to direct prayer to God,
praying that God should give him a worthy guru who
could guide him to God Himself. The prayer, as we all
know, was answered, and Master's contact with Lalaji

was established. The way was at last found, and the quest achieved momentum, culminating in the supreme achievement of *Brahmalaya*.

A yearning for something, we know not what, exists in most hearts. Many of our abhyasis have confided details of their early search. Some were able to find the Master easily, and to come to him quietly with easy and immediate acceptance. Others had to go through long and tedious years of variegated disciplines, often with despair in their hearts, sometimes with danger too, until they came to my Master. Many of the latter have tearfully conceded that their early experiments were unnecessarily prolonged only because they themselves lacked the will and personal courage to abandon a way that had been found unhelpful, and which they knew could not lead them to their chosen destination. What kept them chained to a useless practice was the superstitious fear of possible retribution. It is a deplorable fact that there are gurus who add fuel to the fire of such superstition so as to keep their disciples chained to themselves in permanent bondage for selfish personal gain.

Master teaches that God is simple and therefore the way of attaining Him must also be simple. Master is very often requested to define God, or to describe God, or to give an idea of who or what God is. Master's characteristic answer on every such occasion is, "God is God. What else can be God? Now I tell you one thing. God cannot be known, but he can be experienced." This is a clear indication that knowledge cannot serve us where God is the object or goal of our seeking. The presence of God can be felt, can be experienced by us, and the technique to acquire this experience, to undergo this experience, is what my Master teaches as a practical path.

I remember a discussion about God at Hyderabad many years ago. Master had come to Hyderabad for a short visit. He was accompanied by his permanent companion Shri Ishwar Sahai. Talking about God, Shri Ishwar Sahai tried to show that the difference between man and God is neither one of form, nor of content. He described the difference in terms of purity and subtlety. He used, as an example, the atmosphere covering our earth. "The air at the ground level is the same as that say 50 miles up," he said, "but that near the ground is heavy, dense and impure. As one goes up higher and higher the air becomes purer and purer, and lighter and lighter, until at the very top its qualities are characterised by such purity and lightness that the very existence of air is to be doubted." Using this analogy Shri Ishwar Sahai said, "Man is heavy, gross and impure whereas God is light, pure and subtle." This analogy gives us some idea that qualities or attributes of Divinity do not lie in the physical realm. All that we can do when trying to describe a divine spiritual experience is to use analogies. In the *Bhagavad Gita*, Shri Krishna the *avatar* is himself driven to this contingency. When talking about himself to Arjuna, his devotee, he is forced to use analogies. He says that among rivers he is the Ganga, among birds he is the Garuda, and among men he is Arjuna...and so on! This clearly shows that not even God the Almighty can describe himself. He can however reveal himself to his beloved devotee, as Shri Krishna revealed himself to Arjuna. This draws attention to two important truths of the spiritual search. The first is that God or Reality cannot be known but can be experienced. The second is that this experience itself is

possible only when the Ultimate chooses to reveal itself
to its devotee, or to whomsoever it may choose to reveal
itself. Master has often told me of the great importance
of *attracting* divine grace towards oneself. Master said,
"I am telling you a most important secret. All abhyas is
purely preparatory. Abhyas by itself cannot give anything. It is only a way of turning His benevolent gaze
towards us. Really speaking, only those persons get
divine grace to whom He himself wishes to give it. This
is a great secret I am revealing to you." I asked Master
how to bring this about. How to make the Almighty
Master turn towards us. Master laughed and said, "You
are asking me to reveal to you one more secret. I tell
you this is worth a lakh of rupees! There is only one
way. Love Him so much that He begins to love you.
You must knock on His door so hard that He hears and
opens His door to you. Then your work is over. The
secret is Love. Who can resist it? God is only waiting to
give Himself but it is a pity that no one turns to Him. In
this country the people were known for their spiritual
achievements. Now look at the people. Gross
materialism has taken command over the people. Who
is responsible for this? The people themselves are
responsible for it. They can improve only if they turn
towards Him and adopt the right way of approach. Now
I am telling you another thing. You will find everybody
talking of God. In India it is the biggest topic of conversation and discussion. Everyone talks about God.
Great numbers of books are written about such subjects. Also everybody prays to Him. Then why is there
so much misery and corruption? I will tell you. The approach is wrong. The way of worship has to be
changed."

I requested Master to elaborate a little. "What is it that is wrong with the methods adopted, Master?" I asked. Master replied, "You know the spiritual way. You yourself are following it. Have you not noticed the change in you? You have also had experiences which you have not had before. This you have yourself reported to me. So it is clear, we must follow the right path. I have written in *Reality at Dawn* about this. Now people spend a lot of time and money on gross forms of worship. But what is the use? They become grosser and grosser. It is what is happening. Anybody with eyes can see it. A gross form of worship can only lead to gross results. I have written that God is simple, and therefore the way to achieve Him must also be simple. But people like to follow difficult paths and spend a lot of time and money. Why do they do this? I will tell you. They get satisfaction from such worship. Now look here, people worship for satisfactions! Or if they are a little more developed they may do it to get peace of mind. See how much we have fallen. We do not worship to get God. We worship to get satisfaction or peace of mind, or some such thing. I will tell you another thing. Even a thief prays to his God before leaving his home at night to go for robbery. Look here, he prays to God to help him in this too! I was told that during the war all were praying for success in the war. In England the English people were praying in their churches for victory, while in Germany and Europe they were also praying for their own success in the war. You see this, how prayer is used."

"I have said prayer is begging. In prayer we do nothing else. It is all begging. God give me this, God give me that — it goes on. As we get more we want more, and so this begging is endless. I will tell you an enjoy-

able story. A sannyasi went to the Mughal Court to ask
for some gifts from the Emperor. He was admitted but
told to wait as the Emperor was at prayer. The sannyasi
said he was himself a holy man, and so would like to sit
by the Emperor if this was permissible. He was taken in
and asked to sit outside the prayer room. He heard the
great Emperor praying aloud, 'God give me victory over
my enemies, give me more kingdoms to rule so that
your greatness may be manifested on earth,' and so on.
The sannyasi got up and started walking away. The
Emperor turned round and asked him to wait, saying he
would soon be free as his prayers were coming to an
end. The sannyasi did not heed this but continued on
his way. The Emperor asked him to stop and asked him
why he was going. The sannyasi replied, 'I came to beg
of you for some charity but I find you yourself are begging. What is the use of my begging from another
beggar? I will beg from Him from whom you are begging!' And he departed." Master laughed hilariously
when he concluded this story. Then he became serious
and said, "Even when I joke there is meaning in it. You
see this *tamasha* (joke) of a great Emperor being a
beggar!"

Master continued, "You see, all this is a result of
desires. Our desires have no limit. We get more, and
then we want yet more, and this goes on and on. We
only become bigger beggars, nothing else. So today we
are a nation of beggars. We think of God only when we
want something. God is never thought of for His own
sake. Is this not foolishness? If we have God we will
have everything, whereas when we possess material objects we only possess perishable things. Everything
material will perish. It is only a question of time. We
must look to imperishable things. Desire is not bad. I

have said that *kama* or desire is not bad. Really speaking it is divine. Rather it is Divine creation. *Kama* and *krodha*, love and anger, are both divine. Only our desire must be for God and God alone. Then the desire is used rightly, as a force, to guide us to him. The same power of desire, if wrongly applied towards material possessions takes us away from Him. It is so with all power. Power, by itself, is neither good nor bad. How it is applied or used is what determines the quality of its use. They say power corrupts, but I say power can elevate and liberate us if the power is used rightly. Power, by itself, neither corrupts nor makes us noble. It depends on the way power is used. That is why spiritual power is rarely given to persons until they are purified internally by the methods available in our *sanstha*. This is a very important thing. How can you blame a child if it cuts itself with a knife you have given it? That is why in our *sanstha* there are safeguards against misuse of power. In Sahaj Marg I may say this misuse is impossible. By Lalaji's grace we have a system of training where the abhyasi is purified as he progresses from stage to stage. What does this mean? As a person grows in spirituality he becomes purer too, so that at the highest levels he is absolutely pure. To such persons power can be safely entrusted. They will work under the guidance of the higher consciousness so that wrong use, deliberate or otherwise, is impossible. Normally you will find people applying power out of ego. Then power becomes dangerous. In such cases the power is used for self-importance and not for the good of others. You will see this everywhere. In such persons power of course will corrupt. To tell the truth it will add to the existing corruption. There has been no moral purification, no preparation of the ground. In fact such persons are not to be blamed. They work under the compulsion of their *samskaras*. Really speaking it is the fault of the persons who entrusted power to such people. You see how purity becomes very important for right work. Intelligence, wisdom, all these are good in their own way. They are also necessary up to a point. But purity is essential. Without it no real work can be done. You understand this? And here the heart alone can guide us. Just refer to the heart for guidance and it will give you the answer."

"This is the reason why we start with the heart in our *sanstha*. If the heart is purified then that purity extends throughout the system. The circulation is controlled by the heart. Really speaking this is where the process must really commence. Other points are there as have been taken up by other systems, such as the point of the nose, the point between the eyebrows and so on. But we start with the heart. We take up the heart for our work. Other points for concentration may be good for *siddhis*, for acquiring powers and for limited growth. When we take up the heart under our system we ensure that purification goes on side by side with spiritual progress. This cleaning is very important. Really speaking, at the earlier stages of *sadhana* under our *sanstha* it is very important to do this cleaning regularly. As the purification goes on by removing the impression of past *samskaras*, the possibility of progress is opened up. So this cleaning is very important. You remember the example I gave you of a case where I had to clean the impressions of a previous life? You see how deep these *samskaras* lie? It may be necessary to go back even more. That is why I say a true preceptor or trainer is one who can read the past life. Of course this may not be necessary in every case."

When Master spoke of the safeguards within the system I recalled an experience I had on the 15th February 1967, the day following Vasant Panchami. On Vasant Panchami day I had been granted Provisional Permission by Master to transmit and train people in spirituality. This was at Shahjahanpur. The next day I arrived at Lucknow. One of our abhyasis from Lucknow came to know of my having been granted permission and requested me to give him a sitting. He wanted to be the first person to receive a transmission through me. I agreed, and we sat in meditation. I did not know what to do. I prayed to Master that the transmission may begin and whatever was supposed to happen may happen. After about ten minutes I suddenly had a vision which was as clear as if I was seeing it with my open eyes. I found myself sitting with the abhyasi in front of me. A wall was on my right. It had a door in it, which now opened to admit Master. Master walked through the open door with a chair in his hand, set the chair near me and sat down on it. He then proceeded to keenly observe what I was doing. After some moments the vision vanished. I recalled this to Master and Master said, "Yes, wherever a preceptor may work it always goes on under the Master's supervision. The power itself is the same whether I transmit or some other person transmits, but it is released according to the need of the abhyasi and according to the ability of the preceptor. It is a mighty force, and has to be carefully regulated. But you see it can do no harm. You have seen this yourself."

Master then related to me an experience of his own. Master had been greatly impressed by the love and devotion of one of the abhyasis who was even then a senior preceptor of the Mission. This abhyasi's love attracted Master very strongly towards him, and Master was restless to do something for him. Master said, "This person has great love for me. He is a man of great love and devotion. My heart was restless to give him something. He came to see me when I was at Vijayawada. I asked him to sit in meditation. I wanted to raise him seven points. Look here, seven points!! Do you understand what that means? Several lives are necessary for such progress. But his love was very great and I determined to do it. I moved him up one point, then two points. I had taken him up three points when I heard Lalaji's voice. Lalaji was angry with me. 'What are you doing?' my Master asked me. 'Do you want to destroy him? Stop this nonsense!'" Master laughed and said, "Of course I had to obey the Master. It was a direct order! Now you see the care that Master takes in the work? It is a very potent force, our transmission, and has to be used very carefully. But the checks are there. No harm can ever come from it! Later on the abhyasi wrote to me and said that for one month he had been having headache which was almost unbearable. But you know what he wrote? He wrote to me that even though he was suffering from the headache he prayed to me not to remove it because there was also some enjoyment in it! You see, in my excitement I had done this and it was too much. So Lalaji was taking care. I often do this in my eagerness to prepare persons. But the checks are there. No harm can ever come from it!"

To illustrate that the Master's supervision also works in the other direction of knowing the abhyasi's needs, I relate a personal experience of my own. Master had come to Madras and was staying with his son Chi. Umesh at Besant Nagar. I had gone there one morning to spend some time with him. We were just three or four of us there. Master was preoccupied, morose and

very taciturn. In fact he had been like that for the past
few days and we were all worried about it. He is normally so cheerful and gay and lively that his moodiness
worried us. We had been sitting silently for about an
hour. Suddenly Master got up, with signs of urgency,
and asked me, "Are you free? Can you come inside for a
few minutes?" I was of course free and followed him
into his bedroom. Master closed the door, spread a
bed-sheet on the floor and asked me to sit on it facing
his cot. Then, surprisingly, he himself put on his cap and
sat down in a corner, also facing the cot. Master said,
"Sit in meditation. Lalaji Saheb is here (pointing to the
cot) and wishes to transmit to you!" I was awed, and sat
in meditation. The sitting was one of the briefest, last-
ing hardly 3 minutes. Master said, "That is all," and I
opened my eyes. Master appeared ecstatic. He came to
me and said, "Sabash! I am very happy today. You
know, I have been wanting to do something for you for
the past three or four days, but I did not know how to do
it. I was thinking about this when Lalaji said, 'Why are
you worried about this? If you cannot do it send him in
to me for a few minutes. I shall attend to it myself!'"
Master was immensely pleased. He hugged me and
said, "I am very pleased that you have been able to attract Lalaji's attention towards you. May you grow
spiritually." I was too moved and choked with emotion
to reply. I merely touched his feet in adoration. This
was the first occasion when I had a direct transmission
from Lalaji, the Grand Master. I am relating this to
show that Master's watchfulness is not merely a negative check to prevent misuse of power. It is, on the
contrary, a positive awareness to ensure correct and
timely use of the Divine power for the spiritual benefit
of the abhyasi. This is the sole consideration.

Several years ago I was made to participate in an event which dramatically emphasised this aspect of my Master's work — the care with which an abhyasi is looked after, and his inner needs satisfied. I had gone to Tiruchirapalli on some work and, having completed the work in the forenoon, I had the afternoon to myself. I decided to visit my maternal uncle who was then residing at Tiruvarur, about 50 miles away from Tiruchirapalli. I left Trichy at around 11 o'clock in the morning and arrived at Tiruvarur at 1 p.m. I started to hunt for my uncle's residence, which was not easy as I did not have his address. I had assumed that I would be able to easily locate his residence as I was under the impression that Tiruvarur was a small town. I had not visited Tiruvarur before. However, the job of finding my uncle proved more exhausting than I had expected. After inquiring at half-a-dozen post offices, and after calling at several addresses suggested by the postal authorities, I had to call off the search. I finally decided to leave Tiruvarur as it was already 4 o'clock, and I had to motor a long way back to Madurai.

I left the centre of the small town, and took my road back. While driving through the market place I stopped for a drink as I was feeling very thirsty. I bought a drink from a small betel shop and, while I was drinking it, I was approached by a person whom I did not remember to have met before. He greeted me, and said that he was an abhyasi of the Mission. He said that the whole of the previous night he had felt miserable and abandoned, and that he had spent the whole night weeping and praying for Master's Grace. Even as he was telling me this tears welled up in his eyes. He added, "Sir, you do not remember me. But I have seen you in Trichy two years ago when you came with Master. Here there is no

centre, and I feel totally abandoned. I feel that my tear-
ful prayers of last night have brought you here. I am
grateful to Master for sending you to me. I request you
to kindly come to my room and give a sitting." I accompanied him to his room and gave him a sitting. He was
profusely and sincerely grateful for this sign of Master's
Grace.

After I left him and started on my way back to
Madurai, I thought about this apparently trivial occurrence. I marveled at the whole matter, as it became
evident to me that the whole thing had been planned,
though not by me! The idea came to my mind that
workers of the Mission and of the Master are really like
mobile police squads, who are sent where required. I
had come to Tiruvarur on my personal business, but
Master had diverted me on His! Such is my Master's
love for his abhyasis. This episode revealed to me that
where there is true craving and yearning in the heart of
an abhyasi, the Master's help is ever present, and unfailing in its work.

VIII

The Role of the Guru

The guru occupies and plays a fundamental, decisive and all-pervasive role in the spiritual life of an aspirant. He may appear to be a mere guide playing a limited role at the commencement of practice but, in a perfect and growing guru-disciple relationship, his role becomes greater and greater, and encompasses more and more of the aspirant's life. Finally a culminating spiritual condition is reached where the aspirant's life, in its entirety, is governed and motivated by the guidance of the Master. This is the generally accepted position under Sahaj Marg.

When we study gurus, as such, we find that they range from simple teachers of ritual and scriptural texts at one end of the spectrum to the Supreme Guru of spirituality, one worthy of being called a Master, at the other end. In between these two extremes there are gurus of all shades of practice and precept, filling variegated roles including those of teacher, priest, mendicant, astrologer and so on. Many head organisations of their own, called *mutts*, while a large number are nomadic and wander the length and breadth of the land. The latter are often novices themselves, undergoing prescribed penances and practices in their own search for salvation. But since they wear the ochre robes of the sannyasi they are universally revered as gurus. As a matter of fact the institution of *sannyasa* can often be confusing as far as differentiating between a student and a teacher is concerned. The sannyasis form the bulk of gurus in India. The householder guru is not much in evidence, thanks largely to the teaching of *Advaita Vedanta* which, as interpreted by famous gurus of the past, prescribes celibacy as a rigid pre-condition for embarking on the spiritual quest. It is an important aspect of my Master's teaching that he has set out to make God available to all. And not merely that, my Master teaches that the householder is the person who can be expected to have in him the growing spirit of true spiritual *vairagya* or renunciation. Master has time and again stated that it is in the family environment that true *vairagya* is developed, while performing one's duties. The sannyasi system, on the contrary, encourages runaways and drop-outs, who seek the system merely as a refuge from the demands of a family existence. *Sannyasa* thus encourages weakness, and adds to the already exceedingly large number of itinerant wanderers who live off society without contributing anything significant in return. This is a burden that, in the present context, society can hardly continue to bear, in terms of both materiality and the higher life.

The common run of humanity in India knows that the religious life cannot even be commenced without prescribed initiatory rites being conducted by a priest. Into every individual's life a priest therefore finds entry sooner or later, and thereafter the priest generally becomes the guru of the members of the family which he has summarily adopted. Under the prevailing conditions it is therefore common to find that most persons in India claim a personal guru among their cherished possessions. The guru is rarely changed because of superstitious fears of bad luck, or a fear of being cursed by the rejected guru. Such a guru generally becomes a patiently borne burden, and the religious life degenerates into a hypocritical bargaining game, the householder struggling to minimise his expenses on rituals, while the guru or priest uses all his wit, persuasion and battery of scriptural armaments in an effort to maximise his own income. The family deity is a mute witness to this religious battle of wits conducted in His very presence but, having been imprisoned inside an idol, can say very little about it. There are priests who sincerely believe in the supreme efficacy of rituals, and who perform rituals with complete faith without greed or avarice, but they are few.

All this is somewhat confusing particularly to people from outside India, especially to those on their first visit, who, after studying our literature, come to this country with a pre-established veneration for the institution of gurudom. Most of them are mystified when they find a small fraction of the population claiming to be world-gurus, heads of *mutts*, leaders of cults and sects, and teachers of yoga — and therefore gurus not merely by divine dispensation but in their own right too. The confusion is further magnified when they see even the disciples of such gurus parading as lesser gurus. Such confusion on the part of overseas visitors is not surprising because only a small and minute fraction of the Indian people themselves seems to be aware of the real qualifications a person must possess before he can become a guru. The confusion is so great that mere reciters of prayers, ochre-clad mendicants and astrologers and occasionally even the boss in the office have been adopted as gurus.

The guru is expected to take on the *karmic* burden of any person that he accepts as his disciple. In this *karma*-ridden land, people are generally very anxious to find a guru on whom to dump their accumulated load of *karma*. It would appear that almost anyone willing to accept this burden is therefore acceptable as a guru. People are unwilling to look deeper. There is rarely any positive aspiration to spiritual progress, the attitude generally being merely to get rid of accumulated *karma*. Since the office of guru traditionally carries pecuniary benefits and benefits in kind, the position is really attractive to a large number of persons who easily slip into this role. It is therefore not surprising that gurudom has deteriorated to a mere profession, and not a very noble one at that, attracting the least equipped persons to this high office. The majority are mere tricksters and charlatans who shamelessly deceive a gullible public, aided by a coterie of *chelas* or disciples whose sole duty is to loudly sing the glories of their lord and master while protecting him from the too inquisitive public gaze. This is the level to which this institution, once august, holy and venerated in the highest degree, has now degenerated. Notwithstanding the general corruption and lowering of standards, a few sincere and exalted souls do exist even today, who live disciplined and prayerful lives dedicated to the service of humanity.

However, all this in no degree reduces the real need for a guru of calibre to guide one's spiritual life and to aid in one's development. The need is as imperative as it ever was. But the search for a guru, in modern times, is a long, hazardous and complicated affair, which can even border on heart-break because it is worse than looking for the proverbial needle in the haystack! It is not surprising that many sincere souls have had to waste a considerable portion of their lives in such a search for a real guru.

One of our own associates from abroad told us of the saga of his own personal search, a saga of no mean proportions. He had come to India again and again some six or seven times with the sole intention of searching for, and locating, a person whom he could accept as his guru to guide him on his spiritual journey. On each of these visits he had spent several months visiting ashram after ashram, meeting guru after guru, journeying to holy places one after the other until, in his own words, he could hardly have missed a single ashram or guru of any importance or reputation between the Himalayas and Kanyakumari. His deep sorrow was that in this land renowned for spirituality he could not find one person whom he could whole-heartedly accept as his guru. He was on what he had decided would be his last visit to India, and had again gone around visiting ashrams and gurus. At the end of his travels, just 2 days prior to leaving this country for good, destiny led him to one of our preceptors, and thus his spiritual contact with Master was established. He has indeed been very fortunate in locating his guru, but for every successful search there are literally thousands where the persons have had bitter, frustrating and sometimes even tragic experiences. There are abhyasis with us who have spent a major portion of their lives in the search for a guru, many of whom have suffered loneliness, deprivation, impoverishment and even extreme humiliation before fate gave them the courage to break away and look afresh. Some have related harrowing tales of what happens within the closed confines of some of the 'ashrams', and the personal physical dangers that they had to face when breaking away from them. Some of these escapees have even been threatened with dire consequences if they did not give up their new association with my Master and return to the fold.

As far as finding a real guru of calibre is concerned, there is indeed poverty in this land of plenty, a land replete with gurus.

I had discussed this matter with Master on one occasion, pointing out to him the difficulties many of our abhyasis had to face. Master smiled quietly, but remained silent. I pressed him to say something. Master said, "The real search should be an inner search. A person may go from place to place all over the world, spending his whole life-time, and yet not succeed in finding a guru. The mistake we make is in looking, or searching for a guru. The right way is to **pray** for a guru. What should we do? We should pray direct to God, with deep longing in our hearts, that He may send us a worthy guide. And when we are ready for him the guru will himself knock on our door. I have told you how I got my Master. It is His Grace. So the search should really be one of prayer, an internal search, and then success is assured." This should serve as an eye-opener to all who wish to follow the way of spiritual living and wish to look for a guide for this purpose.

One of our western abhyasis testifies to the efficacy of such an inward, prayerful search. This person had yearned for spiritual growth for many years but had been unable to find anyone to help. The person then fell into a mood of great despondency and despair. The divine spark in the heart was however quite active. The person made a solemn resolve to sit daily in prayer and to pray sincerely for a guru, and to do this exactly for one year. If the prayer should be answered, well and good. If not, well, the very aspiration to follow a spiritual way would be abandoned once and for all. The prayer was sincerely done every day. At this stage, 'miraculously' as the abhyasi said, contact was established with my father who was then in Rome. My father received a letter requesting him to go over to the abhyasi's home-town. How this person came to know of my father's presence in Rome was never divulged — it was, and continues to be, a mystery to him to this day. My father went there, gave this person several sittings, and established a centre of the Mission at that place. This case is a clear and glorious testament to the efficacy of sincere and heart-felt prayer. The guru did come to the person. Agony was there, of course, as this person has told me again and again. But it was a personal and internal agony, cleansing and purifying in nature, capable of orienting the succeeding prayerful state in a definite direction. And success followed quickly. This clearly proves that what my Master told me is possible — if such proof should be needed.

One of the roles of a true guru would therefore appear to be that of awaiting the call of a devoted heart, and responding to it. When one goes deeper into this matter, one finds that even this is a superficial view. What really happens is that Master "prepares the field," as he puts it, by continued work of a spiritual nature. Receptive souls are attracted towards him, and the contact becomes a direct spiritual contact. It would be appropriate to say that the aspirant, ready for the spiritual path, waits at home in a prayerful attitude inviting the guru to come to him. This is the simplest and the best way, as one can rarely know even where to seek the guru, should one set out on a journey to seek him. "All things come to him who waits," says an old proverb, and this applies most pertinently to the coming of a guru into a person's life. The guru, on his part, is putting out spiritual feelers, as it were, and when the feeler finds a receptive person there is information fed back to the

guru. He then commences the preparation of the abhyasi forthwith, by transmission.   Physical contact
between the guru and the disciple may come very much
later.   The exact time of occurrence of the personal
relationship is unimportant in so far as the abhyasi's
preparation is concerned. Frequent personal contact is
largely for the abhyasi's personal satisfaction, and lack
of such personal face-to-face contact in no way inter-
feres with one's progress when one has a Master of
calibre, capable of transmission, and who is himself in
Brahmalaya.

That this is what happens is borne out by Master
himself. Master told me of how he had started ritual
puja, followed by yogic methods and so on, finally praying to God to grant him a capable guru. He came to the
divine feet of Lalaji when he was 22 years old. Some
time later he came to know that Lalaji, wishing to know
who would carry on his work, had meditated on this, and
my Master's face had come up in his vision. Lalaji had
immediately commenced transmission to the person he
had seen in his vision. This was many years before they
met. Master, correlating the times, discovered to his
amazement that the time when Lalaji started transmitting to him coincided with the time when he
commenced his own boyhood prayers in the prescribed
ritual fashion under his mother's guidance. Master told
me, "Had not Lalaji commenced his transmission to me,
even the prayer may not have been performed by me. It
was his transmission which awakened the impulse in
me, and put me on the road to spirituality."

In one of his public lectures at Allahabad, Dr.
Varadachari spoke about this aspect of spiritual life. He
said, "My Master has been able to pick his men from all
strata of society. I say 'pick' even though it seems to us

that we walk in. When we contact him then a direct relationship, after a preliminary cleaning, is effected with the Divine." He also stated in his lecture that Master had told him, "Not only do I choose the man but, having drawn him to me, I give myself unto him." So the very first lesson we learn is that one who is eager to follow a spiritual way of life, and earnestly wants to hand himself over to a guru, should sit in prayer day after day and seek the guru in such prayer to the Almighty. The guru will then come to him when he is ready for him.

This, then, is the very first role of the guru. He prepares the field in such a way that his spiritual power flows into the selected field, finding a place in the receptive hearts of yearning aspirants. In such hearts the power of the Master immediately commences the work of transformation. The aspirant is not aware of this work being done on him. The guru works in secret until the time for a face-to-face meeting between him and the aspirant comes. At this stage the aspirant becomes a disciple, and becomes conscious of the work his Master is doing upon him. The work, so far carried on in secret, now comes out into the open. The seed has germinated underground, and the seedling has now put out its head into the glorious sunshine of the outer world! It is of the nature of cosmic work that creative processes are carried on in secret, away from the prying eyes of all but Mother Nature herself. This appears to be a universal law. When the creative process is completed then only is the result of that work made manifest. Thereafter the process is one of growth. The creative stage is over, the growth stage of the work comes on. This is precisely when the work is brought out into the open. We thus see that the most important aspect of Master's work, the preparation of the field of

the work, and the seeding of the individuals therein, is
carried on in that very secrecy which veils Nature herself!

This explains why my Master's work needs no
publicity or propoganda for its furtherance. He works
alone, using the Divine power placed at his command.
The work is secret in its essential, creative aspect. Not
only is publicity and propaganda unnecessary for this
work, they may very possibly damage it if used in the
early stages of the work. It is worth noting that from the
time Master commences preparing the field, to the time
that the work develops in a public manner, the time in-
terval is, or rather has been in the past, of the order of
20 to 25 years. I would not say this is standard, by any
means. As the work develops it is sure to gain momentum, but the 'visible aspect' of the work, as the earlier
analysis possibly indicates, is the growth stage. It is
therefore only at this stage, when the work has been
revealed to the public gaze, that the question of
publicity invites consideration.

To illustrate this first stage of Master's work I would
like to relate the case of a person who is now a senior
preceptor of the Mission. It was about 15 years ago that
this gentleman read a review of Master's *Reality at
Dawn* in the newspapers. He wrote to Master, evincing
interest in the Sahaj Marg method of yogic training offered by the book. Master replied that his services were
at the disposal of this gentleman, and requested him to
give the method a trial by sitting in meditation. Master
requested this gentleman to give him prior information
as to when he wanted to sit in meditation so that he
could transmit at the appropriate time. Relating this
story this gentleman told me, "When I got Master's letter I decided that while I would sit in meditation I would

not give him prior information about it. After all he claimed to be able to impart the training by transmission. So why should I tell him in advance? In a sense I wanted to test him. Thinking like this I sat down to meditate the very next morning. It was a most wonderful experience. Within moments of my sitting I felt a tremendous power flowing into my heart. It was as if molten lead was being poured into me." This gentleman realised that Master was not dependent on his information to commence his work. His divine work had commenced much earlier. It was only necessary for the abhyasi to feel it by an act of conscious participation in the work.

In a sense this first stage is the most important stage of Master's work. In another sense it is also perhaps the stage which is easiest for him. At this level of functioning there is no resistance because the aspirant, being unaware of the work being done on him, cannot offer any resistance to the work. There is no conscious receptivity or co-operation called for since the aspirant is ignorant of the Master working upon him. His own yearning or craving acts as a powerful force which attracts Master's Grace into him, and this alone acts as the strong co-operative factor in enabling Master to work on him. The conscious wielder of spiritual power, the Master, has a degree of co-operation from his unknowing partner, the aspirant, which he but rarely receives in the later stages of his work. Once the Master's relationship with the aspirant becomes formalised and assumes the guru-disciple relationship the work comes out into the open. Then his problems really start. It is now that the disciple can resist the Master's work, consciously or otherwise. At this stage the disciple is aware of the fact that he is being worked upon. He begins to question the efficacy of the power, of the existence of the power, then the source of that power itself. He perhaps also begins to doubt the Master's ability. And so it goes on, doubt upon doubt, and then resistance grows. We see that at the conscious level the resistance can be considerable. Yet it is not very difficult for the Master to overcome this resistance because conviction can be brought to the abhyasi by reasoning, by example and by asking him to observe the result of Master's work upon him. A degree of trust can thus be created which, as the work progresses from one level of consciousness to higher levels, from one level of being to yet higher levels, develops into faith, then into love, culminating finally in surrender. If, however, the resistance is subconscious then the work can be much more difficult and prolonged.

Master has aptly and graphically divided aspirants into two classes. One class is apparently highly co-operative at the conscious level, but the resistance is all inside, hard as a rock, and this class Master compares to the mango fruit which has a soft, pulpy exterior, but a hard stone inside. The other class of abhyasis are externally and consciously tough. It would appear that they do not agree with anything the Master says or does. Resistance appears to be considerable. Yet, inside, the co-operation is something extra-ordinary. Such individuals are compared to the almond which has a hard shell on the outside but a soft, sweet kernel inside.

If one is observant one can see this division among abhyasis clearly. There are abhyasis who are very pliant and soft, and apparently co-operate in the highest degree, but who make very slow progress, and in certain cases none at all. They stick on to the system year after year. In one such case I have even felt that a degree of injustice was being done to the abhyasi. He had been in the Mission for many years even when I first met him, but I found Master always very critical when talking to him. It was when I asked Master why such an apparently co-operative soul was being treated somewhat harshly that Master explained this point to me. "Look here," he said, "He is very soft and says he has surrendered completely to me. But inside he is like a rock. There is stubborn inner resistance. I have tried to help him but the transmission will not enter his heart. His heart is closed up. It is just reflected back. You see the problem? How to help such a person? It can be done but it is a very long process, and he has to be patient and try to create co-operation within himself." I was somewhat taken aback by this explanation. I asked Master how this sub-conscious resistance came up all of a sudden, particularly when the craving was strong enough to have brought him to Master. I could well understand that conscious resistance could crop up in one type of abhyasi. This is a normal occurrence in inter-personal relationship, and one which is easy to understand. But how could sub-conscious resistance crop up of a sudden? This was my perplexity. Master said, "I use the word sub-conscious merely as a common usage of this term to indicate that it is a state of mind of which the abhyasi is not aware or conscious. I don't like to use the word 'unconscious' because that has a different meaning altogether, though it is not really incorrect. I will explain it in a different way. It is the *samskaras* which are creating this resistance. Sometimes the *samskaras* are so deep that they are difficult to overcome. Regular cleaning is necessary for a long time. This is the effect of *samskaras* — I mean this resistance. So you see, such persons have to be patient and try to create co-operation. There is one further difficulty. On the superficial or conscious level they are very anxious for development. But there should be no anxiety. Anxiety means doubt is combined with it. Craving is what is needed. A single-minded longing for realisation is what is needed. But these people mistake the surface anxiety for craving and co-operation, and so change of attitude becomes very difficult to bring about. When I tell them this thing, generally the resistance is further increased. Now what can I do? So I work in my own way — of course time will be taken for it."

This brings us to the second stage of Master's work — cleaning and purifying the abhyasi to make quick progress possible, and to consolidate that progress. What is it that is cleaned? Master's general answer is that the whole system has to be thoroughly cleaned. This includes the heart and the higher points one after the other. The main work is on the heart and the heart region where much of the *samskaric* residue lies buried in the form of grossness. Master teaches that when we act in any way — the word 'act' being taken in its widest meaning to include all sensory activity and mental activity — the action leaves an 'impression' which is called a *samskara* when it is very deep. It is clear that the superficial impressions are easily cleaned off. It is easy to wipe a slate and clean it. But it is not so with a gramophone record, for instance, where the impressions have been made deep enough to form permanent grooves. When we become 'involved' in our actions the danger of deep impressions being formed is much greater. The accumulated impressions which are in us form the *samskaric* burden of the past. This has to be cleaned by the Master by the use of his own spiritual power. As this cleaning proceeds the abhyasi experiences actual 'lightness' during his meditation sittings.

I had a personal problem in this connection which I once discussed with Master. When I first started meditation a great number of thoughts used to come up and intrude but, on following Master's technique of not attending to thoughts, the inrush of thoughts became progressively reduced until I could experience intervals of thoughtlessness. But, and this was my problem, after a few years of *sadhana* I suddenly found thoughts of a most sordid and vile nature coming during meditation. Naturally I was considerably perturbed because I was apprehensive that this might indicate not progress but regress. Master quickly cleared the problem up for me. He said, "You see, the dust that settles every day on the table can be easily dusted off. It is superficial and easy to remove. Suppose ink has been poured on the table and allowed to soak, then the cleaning is more difficult. So the nature of the impression makes the difference. Now I tell you one more thing. We sometimes have bad thoughts, I mean consciously. We feel ashamed and push them down. Now the very bad or worst thoughts are hidden away deep inside the mind. So in cleaning they may come up last of all. In your case this is what has happened. You should be happy that these vile thoughts have been removed at last. Progress will be quicker now. Do you understand this? It is like a pond. The leaves and dust float on its surface and can be easily removed. But heavy dirt sinks down, and effort is necessary. So in cleaning it comes up last. So there is nothing to worry about. But I am telling you it is important to remove the day's accumulation the same day itself. Otherwise tomorrow it will have become a little more hard and solid, and require more effort. That is why I prescribe daily cleaning by the abhyasis themselves. This process, if correctly followed, will remove the day's accumulation. The rest is the Master's work. So you see the importance of daily cleaning?"

On one occasion, several years after I had commenced *sadhana*, I went to Shahjahanpur. Master had been telling me that my progress was good and that he was generally very satisfied with it. He gave me an individual sitting which lasted over half-an-hour. At the end of it he said, "Now I have cleaned your system and removed the grossness." I was a bit perturbed to hear this because I felt that there could not be much need for cleaning. I told Master that I had done nothing consciously which could have added grossness to my system. He had also been writing to me praising my progress. I requested him to explain how this grossness had now come into me to need cleaning. Master laughed and said, "You should not worry about this. It was not much, but you know I am a perfectionist and I cannot bear to see even a single dark spot in the system. I will tell you one thing. On a black shirt a dirty patch or spot will not show, but on a clean white shirt even the smallest drop of ink will stand out and invite attention to itself. Anyway it is my concern and you should not worry about it." But I pressed Master for an answer as to how this grossness came into being. Master replied, "However pure our action, some impression is always there. This is inevitable at the human level. I also get grossness, which my Master cleans whenever necessary. Another thing I am telling you. When we sit in meditation there is a craving in the heart for something. This creates a vacuum, and grossness from the surrounding atmosphere is attracted and becomes deposited on us. A person who is meditating properly therefore accumulates some grossness like this also. That is why if there is one saint of calibre in a country it is enough. He attracts all the grossness of the whole place and takes it upon himself. That is why I have said that a saint is the target for the world's sorrows! I will tell you another thing which is very surprising. Grossness can actually come from the parents and forefathers too! I have found this in several cases, where the grossness has been handed down like that. So you see, this can happen in several ways but you should not worry about it." This ended the discussion.

At a subsequent discussion Master emphasised the importance of cleaning as related to progress. Master said, "By Lalaji's Grace we have a method of training which I can say is of unsurpassed efficacy. Do you know what makes it such a wonderful and easy system? It is the cleaning process followed under Sahaj Marg. Really speaking it is our past impressions which hold us down and create patterns of behaviour which we are unable to modify. We are the slaves of our past. We think we are free to think and act as we like but, truly speaking, this is a fallacy. We are conditioned in everything by the past. Now how to change a person under these conditions? This is Lalaji's greatness that by this process of cleaning he makes it possible to completely remove the effects of the past, in stages of course. You see what a great boon this is. What is the use of telling a person he must change? Of course everyone would like to change, but it is not possible. Why? Because the mind is conditioned by the past. So you see, change can come only by cleaning the mind of past impressions. This makes it possible for the abhyasi to be slowly liberated from his past. Really speaking this is our only bondage. Our past impressions create tendencies in us which we find difficult to change. When the impressions are cleared, the tendency can be changed easily and, in many cases, automatically. Then thought and action become correct and natural. Therefore to transmit is not enough. Cleaning is very important. Otherwise the abhyasi may progress but the danger of fall is always there because the impressions of the past can drag him back. If progress is to be made permanent, purification of the system is essential. That is why I ask our preceptors to pay more attention to this aspect of the work. It is a very important aspect. But much hard work is necessary particularly at the lower stages. So sometimes there is a tendency to ignore this, but then that is a dis-service to the abhyasi. We are here to serve the abhyasi, and if cleaning is neglected then we are not really serving him. This I tell again and again to our preceptors."

This subject of cleaning crops up again and again in my discussions with Master. It is a process to which he gives the greatest importance, and to which he also ascribes great efficacy. At one such discussion session I asked Master how long this need for cleaning would exist. Master laughed and said, "This depends on you. If there is complete co-operation then the work is easy. Suppose I go on cleaning and the abhyasi goes on adding more and more grossness, than what can I do? So you see the abhyasi must co-operate too. He must modify his life in such a way that it is helpful to his progress. To remove past accumulations is the Master's work. But the abhyasi should be alert that he does not add more grossness by his own thoughts and actions. So this alertness is necessary. And if the daily process of self-cleaning is followed, then by Lalaji's grace a stage can be reached when the formation of impressions no longer takes place, and samskara formation stops. This is a very high stage, but really speaking it is but the start of the journey. Once *samskara* formation stops then the goal is in sight. The past accumulations may be there, some residue of it, but that is Master's responsibility. But I tell you one more thing. As long as we are in this body some grossness will always be there. If the system becomes completely pure then life cannot remain here. But (laughing) we should not create grossness in ourselves to prolong our lives! But when *samskara* formation stops it is a sign that the goal is coming near us. Then the person lives and works normally in every way but no impressions are formed. This is the condition which I have called the 'living dead!' But to arrive at this condition the abhyasi must co-operate. How to do this? I will tell you. Suppose I see a beautiful rose, I admire it. There is nothing wrong in it. But I must not look at it again and again and create strong impressions of its beauty. Then the impression forms on the mind. If the impression is strong enough we want to go back again and see it, and this further strengthens the impressions. Then the desire to possess it comes into play, and if we yield to it, action begins. So you see a simple thought, if allowed to go on unchecked, can lead on and on to action, and then its result, I mean the result of that action, must inevitably follow. So a train of events is set up and we are caught up in it. That is why we must be very alert."

Master has clarified that by impressions he means both good and bad ones. Good impressions are no better than bad ones. Both are equally undesirable as they create impediments to progress. This is a pointer to an important aspect of Master's teaching. A good life, one that has been conducted on principles of good conduct, charity, adherence to religious codes etc., is not suffi-

cient to make 'spiritual progress' possible. For this
something more than a life of mere social and ethical
goodness is necessary. All these form *samskaras*. Such
a life may grant a better future life, but our aim is liberation. So all these concepts are of no value to the abhyasi
under the Sahaj Marg system. To what ultimate levels
this applies was revealed to me when I once discussed
the religious practice of reciting sacred *mantras* into the
ears of a dying person. Such *mantras* are called *karna
mantras* and are said to be highly effective in guiding the
departing soul on its onward journey to its goal. The
mantras are said to work even if spoken into the ears of
an unconscious person who is dying. The only stipula-
tion is that the person be not dead. I asked Master
about this. Master became pensive. He said, "Because
you are asking me sincerely I will tell you. There is no
use in this for spiritual progress. Yes, it may grant the
person a better re-birth, but what is the use of that? Our
idea is not to be reborn, however good the next life may
be. Our aim is liberation. Now I am telling you the correct thing. At death the mind should be made a
complete blank. No thoughts must be allowed to come
into it, not even of gods or anything like that. It must be
made completely blank so that at death it can merge
with the Source where the condition is that of nothing-
ness. And I tell you, for the abhyasis of our *sanstha* this
is very easy because this is what they are taught to do
every time they sit in meditation. To us this becomes
second nature. When we sit in meditation the mind becomes thoughtless, and so what we are experiencing, to
put it in one way, is a condition somewhat like that at
death. You may call it a condition of death-in-life if you
like. So when the time comes we automatically get into
this state of mind, and there is no impediment even at

the last moment. Now you see how much harm this *karna mantra* can do? It is actually a method of dragging the soul back to this existence instead of allowing it to go on its way. If I tell this to the pundits they will pounce upon me! But this is the correct thing that I am telling you."

That the cleaning is not confined to the individual human system has already been apparent. A saint 'attracts' grossness from the atmosphere onto himself. He acts like a cosmic vacuum cleaner. So cleaning of the atmosphere is another important aspect of Master's work. As the environment is so purified the effect on people's minds is significant. Right thoughts come to people's minds, and so pure actions, or right actions, follow naturally. Thus by acting on a cosmic level the individual is benefited. In turn as the individual's spiritual condition improves he affects the environment. And so this goes on. What began at the cosmic level as field preparation culminates once again in the cosmic level after having gone through the level of the individual. What happens to all the grossness cleaned off in the process? Preceptors are instructed only to remove it and throw it out. What then happens to this? Is there any way of destroying this? This was the question I asked Master. Master answered that such grossness could be burnt up, but only the Special Personality could do it! The Special Personality alone has the power necessary to burn it up and destroy grossness. All others can only remove it and throw it out somewhere.

Growth has to be nourished. There can be no growth without proper nourishment. This is the third role of the Master, that he 'feeds' the abhyasis with his spiritual transmission and nourishes them, so that growth continues to be strong and healthy. What we call transmission Master once defined as 'spiritual food.' The body lives and grows at the physical level, and so sustains itself on physical foods. The soul, being spiritual in nature, needs food of that plane. I once asked Master whether the transmission was the same in quality or whether it differed with the abhyasi's condition. Master answered that there could be no change in it as it is the subtlest force or power of Divinity, and hence unchanging. I was a bit puzzled as to how the same power could do everything Master claimed it could achieve, at all levels of development. I put this question to Master. Master laughed amusedly and said, "When we plant a seed we water it; when it comes up as a small seedling we water it; when it is a strong plant we water it; and we go on watering it all its life. The same water achieves the growth of the plant stage after stage."

On a different occasion Master described transmission in terms other than what I have stated above. He said, "The body is alive only because the soul is in it. At death the soul flies away, and then we say the person is dead, and call the body a corpse. So the body lives by the soul. How does the soul live? I will tell you. The soul lives by transmission which we can think of as the essence of Divinity. Dr. Varadachari has called this 'Soul of the soul.' It is a correct description that he has given. He told me in Sanskrit it is *pranasya pranaha* which means the soul of the soul. So, really speaking, without transmission the soul is like a dead thing. The very first transmission makes the soul alive. It is the touch of Divinity itself. I am telling you a wonderful thing. Even a single transmission can make a great difference in a person's future. One transmission from a Master of calibre can transform a person instantly. The power is the same. But the will must be there. **There**

must be an unfailing will. Then the result is wonderful. Really speaking this is the most important thing, that a trainer in spirituality must possess an unfailing will. I am telling you one more thing. When we doubt the efficacy of the power of transmission it really means we are doubting our Master. Then the work suffers. The power can be given by the Master, but you have to develop will power yourself. After all, in using any instrument force has to be applied. Suppose you want to cut wood and I give you a saw. The saw has to be moved with the full force of your arm. Then only will it cut the wood. Do you follow this? So an instrument alone is not sufficient. You have to use the force of your will to make it work effectively. Really speaking whether I transmit or a preceptor transmits, the result should be the same. But if will is not behind the transmission then the work is not properly done. So the abhyasi feels the difference."

The transmission is thus the only spiritually elevating power. This enables the abhyasi to grow from stage to stage, passing through region after region of spiritual existence, and so on to the Goal. Right through this divine journey the Master's active help and guidance are essential. This is unique in Sahaj Marg that the guru's role lasts until the abhyasi has been taken up to the highest level of spiritual existence open to mankind. In fact the need for the guru is progressively more as we grow. Master once explained why this is so. Master said, "As the abhyasi grows, the transmission and cleaning make yet higher approaches open to him. But at the higher approaches a resistance develops from above. It is as if nature opposes his development. Here the Master has to use the power at his disposal to take the abhyasi to the higher level. The abhyasi by himself can-

not undertake this. There are certain regions where the
abhyasi cannot even enter by himself. I will tell you one
more thing. There are regions which no person can
cross by himself. Only a capable guide who is in *laya*
with the Ultimate, and who has travelled the path himself, can do it. At such stages the Master takes the
abhyasi *inside himself* and crosses the region, and then
brings the abhyasi out again to continue the journey
under Master's guidance and supervision. Dr.
Varadachari used to joke about this and say, 'The
Master is like a kangaroo!' You know, the kangaroo has
a special pouch into which it puts the baby kangaroo
when there is any danger. So this is what the Master has
to do for his abhyasi whenever it becomes necessary."
This exposes to our understanding yet another role of
the Master, that of protector.

We thus arrive at a broad understanding of Master's
several roles which are those of field preparation, seeding of the individual's heart, nourishing the growth of
the abhyasi, and protecting him on his spiritual journey
until the goal is in sight. At this stage the abhyasi, according to Master, should have crossed into the central
region, and also crossed several rings of the seven rings
of splendour in that region. The Master takes him yet
further until all the rings are crossed. After this nothing
remains but to swim on and on towards the Centre in
what Master calls the Ocean of Bliss. According to
Master, at this stage the abhyasi is put in direct contact
with God. In so far as the abhyasi is concerned, this then
is the culmination of the Master's role in his *sadhana*.

I however believe that even though the abhyasi may
now be in direct contact with God his relationship with
the Master does not cease to exist since, by its very nature, it is a spiritually and eternally enduring one.

I recently discussed this aspect of an abhyasi's link with the Master even after the Master has connected him to God. Master was not willing to give a direct answer, but suggested that at this stage it was up to the abhyasi to retain his link with the Master, or to go on by himself. Master said, "For those who need the Master's help even beyond that stage it is always available." With this pregnant statement he became silent! Sister Kasturi was present. She told me that even at the highest stages of spirituality the possibility of ego developing could not be ruled out. And the direct link with God, established for the abhyasi by the Master, could lead to ego if the abhyasi was not careful and level-headed. "After all, how is the direct connection with God established?" she asked. "It is by the Grace of the Master alone that this is possible. So how does the question of severing one's link with the Master ever arise? I feel that when Master makes such a statement to an abhyasi, he is really testing the abhyasi. At this stage we have to be extremely cautious and see that we do not indulge in the supreme mistake of abandoning Master." She then related to me a vision of hers relating to this subject. On one occasion Master had told her that a certain abhyasi had been connected direct to God. However, when she studied the matter, it appeared to her in her vision that as the soul of the abhyasi approached God, it was thrown back to Master. When the soul of the abhyasi strove to approach God once again, the same thing was repeated — the soul was thrown back to the Master. Sister Kasturi said, "See, brother, this was a direct revelation that the Master's role never ends; not even after an abhyasi's link with God is established! Because the journey to the Goal is, in a sense, an endless one. We are always approaching the Centre, coming nearer and nearer to it, but we can never be at the Centre itself. That can happen only at the time of *mahapralaya* when everything is drawn back into the Centre."

My own belief is that if an abhyasi has sincerely and devotedly loved the Master, then there can never be any thought of cutting his link with the Master. The true connection with Master is therefore an eternal one, whatever stage of spiritual growth the abhyasi may have attained, since the need for Master's help and guidance is ever present.

IX

Spiritual Experiences

My Master teaches that few spiritual experiences have real significance and therefore undue importance should not be attached to them as this may divert us from our goal. Persons who give too much importance to experiences are likely to 'miss the wood for the trees.' Too much importance has been given to dreams, visions, hearing of voices and the like in the traditional works on the subjects of religion, yoga and mysticism. This has led aspirants to wrongly conclude that where there are no such experiences, something is seriously wrong with their practice of the method. My Master has emphatically stated that experiences, as experiences, have no value since what should concern us is the attainment of the Goal, and not experiences en route. We may take note of them in the same manner as we note the passing landscape when on a journey. No greater importance should be attached to them. In any case, a desire or craving for experiences is definitely a wrong attitude, and should be changed forthwith.

On one occasion when Master was at Hyderabad, an eager group of persons was around him, asking questions. One young man asked this question about the validity of spiritual experiences. Master gave his usual answer, that we should not worry about them. The abhyasi however pressed for an answer, asking whether such experiences did not denote stages on the journey, and thus were indicators of how far the journey had been completed. As an analogy he said, "Sir, when I travel from here to Bombay by train, the stations on the way come in a particular order. So by knowing which station we have arrived at I can judge how near I am to my destination. Surely spiritual experiences have a similar value." Shri Ishwar Sahai who was present smiled and said, "What you say is true if I go by train. Suppose I travel by air, then how am I to judge what stages of the journey have been completed? We have then to rely on the captain of the plane to tell us where we are, and how much farther we have to go to reach our destination. Even when the captain tells us where we are the information may convey nothing to us. So this question is to be answered like this." The questioner laughed and said, "Yes, I see the point. You take us by air..!"

Speaking in a very general manner, experiences can be classified as falling into three groups. The first group contains experiences arising out of the abhyasi's own imagination, or as a result of his having projected them himself. Abhyasis, indeed all human beings, are prone to discuss matters among themselves, and to exchange notes on each other's experiences. In spiritual *sadhana* this is not advisable since, in the same sitting, different abhyasis may undergo different experiences. This does not mean that one is progressing more, or faster, than another. Experiences depend on such diverse factors as the *samskaras* of the individual, his previous background, social environment and so on. If abhyasis discuss each other's experience, some may feel that they are not getting the right experience from meditation, and may feel dejected. Worse, they may project the same things unconsciously during subsequent sittings and have experiences which are their own creation. Therefore Master advises abhyasis not to discuss their

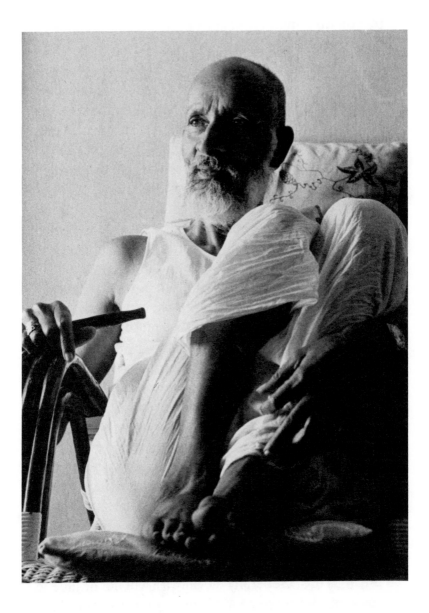

spiritual experiences with each other, but only with
Master himself or with the preceptor. Such experiences
are not true spiritual experiences and have no value
whatsoever.

The second group covers all experiences arising
from the cleaning process. Master has stated that when
the system of the abhyasi is cleaned, then the past impressions are removed. When these impressions
surface to the mind then the original experience or activity which created the impressions is once again
created in the mind. So the abhyasi has an 'experience.'
In general the experiences which abhyasis have are of
this category. The visions of gods and goddesses that
abhyasis experience during meditation are of this type.
Whenever such an experience comes up, it is an indication of a past involvement with that particular deity. I
have referred elsewhere to one such experience where
Master himself saw a monkey in the place of an abhyasi.
Many abhyasis have startlingly clear visions of gods or
saints. Quite a few make the tragic mistake of thinking
that the goal has been reached, since their chosen personal god has granted them his *darshan*. It is a pity that
persons who practise without the guidance of a capable
Master mistake such experiences for divine revelations,
and go back to the traditional forms of worship of that
particular deity which appeared to them. Abhyasis have
to be on their guard against such misinterpretation of
experiences. Many abhyasis report having visions of
gardens, hill-stations and the like. These also belong to
the same category. Some experiences may also refer to
a previous life. Generally the abhyasi will not be able to
know this. But Master and the preceptors will be able to
correctly interpret and evaluate such experiences, par-

ticularly if they have occurred during sittings with the Master or the preceptor.

The third category contains what Master has referred to as "revelatory experiences." These are of a very valuable nature as they contain messages from the inner Self of the abhyasi which, if properly interpreted, can help him considerably on his journey. Such experiences may come during meditation sittings, or as dreams. Master has also stated that orders, instructions, and advice from the Master himself can be conveyed in this way.

Some eight months after I commenced the practice of meditation under the Sahaj Marg system, I had a dream. In the dream there was a narrow river, with a tarred road beside it. On the other side of the road, away from the river, was a large hall. I went up the steps and found an enormous quantity of footwear lying outside the door. I inferred that there was a large gathering inside. In the next scene I found Master coming out of this hall. I joined him. Both of us walked up the road along the river. We came to a narrow bridge spanning the river. We got on to it to go across, and just as we were halfway across I bent down and touched his feet. This dream was the cause of immense satisfaction to me. At the conscious level I had fully accepted my Master. This dream now confirmed that at the subconscious level too there had been an acceptance of the Master, and so my acceptance of him was now total. I accepted this dream as revealing an inner condition.

A few years later I had a period of depression which lasted about three months. During this period I could not meditate satisfactorily and, if I remember right, I had stopped meditating for some time. At the peak of this depression I arrived in Bangalore on an official visit. Before going to bed I prayed to Master, telling him that I was unable to help myself in any way, and that it was now up to him to put me back on the path from which I seemed to be straying. I prayed for his guidance and assistance to find the way again. I slept very deeply that night. I woke up as usual at about 5 a.m. but strange to say, I went to sleep again, and slept very deeply. During this second sleep I had a dream. I dreamt I was in a large compound. I entered a large building half of which was an open courtyard, where several women seemed to be cutting and preparing vegetables for cooking. The other half was covered. I entered it. It was in total darkness. At one end there was a raised dais, and on it was seated a person whom I could not as yet see. As I looked at him some illumination began to glow behind him. I saw his silhouette. Slowly the light became stronger, and I saw Lalaji sitting on the dais, a radiant smile on his beautiful face, his beard illuminated by the light from behind him, wearing a shawl around his shoulders. I stood mute before him. Lalaji spoke to me. He said, "So far you have been meditating in one way. I shall now teach you another method. Meditate on my form as that from which the entire manifested Universe has been created." Though Lalaji spoke, the voice I heard was that of my Master Babuji Maharaj. As soon as I woke up I sat in meditation, meditating as advised for over an hour. The meditation was very deep and I was in a condition like that of *samadhi*. My depression vanished. It was as if a new beginning was made. When I reported this experience to Master he exclaimed, "You have had a wonderful experience. A secret has been revealed to you. You know what it is? It has been revealed to you that my Master and I are one, though people see us as separate beings."

Perhaps a year later I had another vivid dream. I dreamt that I was taking evening group meditation in a thatched pavilion with only the roof to it. There were no walls on any side, only poles to hold up the roof. It was twilight, and getting dark. I closed my eyes and started the sitting. A few moments later I had the feeling that all the abhyasis who had been meditating had got up and were moving around. I opened my eyes, and saw that all the abhyasis were indeed moving around but all had their eyes closed. Each one had a dagger in his hand which he was trying to plunge into me. I was frightened and shouted, "Master! Master!" At this stage I woke up. I referred this to Master. Master said, "It is a good dream. It is an indication that the lower vrittis are being destroyed. It is a sign for further progress."

When we analyse the situation we discover an important trend. The imaginary experiences and those projected by the abhyasi himself, come very early in a person's spiritual life and, fortunately, do not last long. The experiences arising out of cleaning may be numerous, and may last for many years depending on the condition of the abhyasi. The revelatory experiences come when the abhyasi is established on the path, and devotion for the Master has filled his heart. There is no set time for this. It may be the very same day on which one commences abhyas, or never at all.

Apart from these experiences there are those that can be created by the power of the transmission itself, when consciously done with such an intention. I recall going to Dr. Varadachari at Madras one hot summer evening for a sitting. When I reached his residence I was hot and sweating profusely. Within minutes of my arrival he asked me to sit with him in meditation. I continued to feel very hot as the fan was not on. But, strange to say, within two or three minutes of commencing meditation I felt a cool breeze blowing around me. I cooled off immediately. The breeze continued to blow, and I actually felt a little chilly. At the same time I could feel that the atmosphere around me was still as hot as ever. I was puzzled, but enjoyed the cool breeze that seemed to be blowing for my benefit. When the sitting ended Dr. Varadachari asked me what I had felt. I told him of the peculiar sensation. He bellowed with laughter. His eyes had a mischievous twinkle in them. "See," he said, "That is the beauty of this system. I knew you were feeling hot and so I transmitted to you from the water centre. So you felt cool and refreshed. A capable preceptor must be able to work upon the system as a musician plays upon an instrument!"

I heard of a second instance from Master himself. It was in the early days of his *sadhana*. He wanted to try the effects of different levels of transmission. He transmitted to an abhyasi from a particular centre which would produce signs of intoxication. Master said, "Now look here, when the sitting was over this abhyasi could hardly get up. He had all the signs of drunkenness upon him. He was completely intoxicated. This was transmission of a low, material order. This should not be done as there is no benefit to the abhyasi. We must always transmit from as subtle a level as possible."

A third occasion relates to my father. He had a hankering to visit the holy shrine at Badrinath. He had had this desire ever since his boyhood. We had arrived at Shahjahanpur to attend the wedding of Master's son Chi. Umesh. My father expressed a desire to go from there to Badrinath, and sought Master's permission. Master said, "Why do want to go there? It is dangerous. The roads are bad and a journey now is a great risk. If you are hankering for the experience you hope to get there, sit in meditation and I will give you the experience here itself right now. There is no need to undertake such a troublesome and risky journey for this purpose!" The implications of this are tremendous. I will relate one particular example to show at what levels such experiences can be imparted to a disciple if Master desires to do so. There had been a lot of new thinking about the moon, several years before moon travel was even contemplated in the West. Our sister Kasturi had expressed a desire to know what conditions were like on that satellite. Master said, "All right. Sit in meditation. I will try to give you the experience of that condition." Sister Kasturi told me that she did have a profound experience and had noted the details down in her diary. Later visits to the moon by the American astronauts revealed certain conditions which she had experienced many years earlier.

We thus see that one more order of spiritual experience is now introduced into the picture. We have to reclassify the subject of spiritual experiences into two major classes. The first one consists of all those experiences that an abhyasi experiences by himself during his meditation, with or without preceptors, as well as in dreams. This class is amenable to the three-fold subdivision I have referred to earlier. The second major class contains all experiences which the Master deliberately induces in us, or makes possible for us to experience. Such experiences can be of any level of 'being'. I recall our preceptor, Shri S.K. Rajagopalan, telling me many years ago, of an occasion when a high-ranking official visited my Master. This official desired to be enlightened on various topics. At the end he asked Master what the state of *jivan mukti* was. Master answered that he could not explain or describe this state but could enable the official to experience it if he so desired. The official said, "I see," and went away. Shri S.K. Rajagoplan used to bewail the ignorance of that official which deprived him of a heaven-sent opportunity for immediate grace being bestowed on him. Who can enter such a state, even if it is only for a moment, and ever be the same again? The experiences Master bestows on us are of this order where each such experience raises us to levels of 'being' impossible for us to attain by our own effort. Such experiences are not mere experiences. They are moments of grace and bliss when the abhyasi basks in the infinite love of the Master.

X

The Gift of Liberation

The ultimate aim of *sadhana* under the Sahaj Marg system of raja yoga is rather loosely designated as being liberation or realisation. These two terms are generally used interchangeably, as if they were synonymous, and represented the same condition or state of Being. Those closer to Master, who have had more experience of Master's use of the terminology of his system, appreciate that there is not merely a difference between these two words, but the difference is indeed a large and significant one. Sometimes a third term is used, this being 'the perfect human condition' or the 'condition of the perfect human being.' Thus the goal is generally described in these terms, the exact term used depending on the person's degree of intimacy with Master, and his own growth and experience in the system.

As far as I have been able to understand this subject, it appears to me that liberation is a lesser order of attainment when compared to realisation. In Sahaj Marg terms liberation is indeed of a far higher level than the traditional religious emancipation labelled *mukti* or *moksha*, both of which generally refer to a state of salvation from which there is no return to the physical plane of existence. They, however, do not preclude rebirth in higher non-physical realms of existence, of which Master says there are many. So *mukti* and *moksha* are limited concepts, whereas the liberation of Sahaj Marg yoga offers a permanent release from the chain of births and deaths.

There is a more significant difference. Traditional religion seems to provide, by and large, for release only after death. This is called *videha mukti,* that is *mukti* after one has vacated the body. The *jivan mukta* state, that is the state of release in this life itself, while one is yet alive, is stated to be a very high order of *mukti,* possible only to a very few. Under Sahaj Marg the emphasis is on the attainment of liberation in this life itself, here and now, while one is living a normal life as a householder.

My Master effects the transformation of the abhyasi by using the Divine force and infinite power available to him. This power is used to awaken the dormant spiritual forces in the person of the abhyasi. By this process, coupled with the process of cleaning, this physical body is slowly transformed by breaking up every atom and reconstituting it until, finally, no tinge of materiality exists in it. For all practical purposes it is a physical, material body both in appearance and function, but in reality it is now a pure spiritual body. Such a pure body is said to be beyond the five *koshas* or sheaths. Such a body alone can be the body of a liberated soul. Persons who have attained this state under my Master's guidance are said to possess such bodies. Such a liberation, where a liberated soul occupies a spiritualised, divinised body and continues to live out its allotted span of earthly existence, is what is offered by my Master. We don't have to wait for death to be liberated. This may have been necessary under other disciplines where the vehicle of the soul, the body, could not be purified and divinised to contain a liberated soul. But my Master is able to reconstitute the gross physical body by working on what, for the lack of a better expression, can be called the atomic level into a new spiritual body. This he does by the power of his transmission.

When I requested Master to give a short definition of liberation, Master said, "In one who has been liberated what is first broken is 'time'. Time is destroyed first." This is clear enough as far as it goes, implying that one who is liberated is no longer subject to the sway of time. For such a person all temporality ceases to exist, and one steps into eternity. I have long tried to understand this concept of eternity. The only clear understanding I have arrived at is that eternity does not mean unlimited extension in time. It seems to be of a different order of existence. My understanding today is no whit better than when I started meditation under my Master ten years ago. But on one occasion I had an experience of eternity which I can never forget. It was towards the end of 1968. I had gone to Shahjahanpur to be with Master for a couple of days while I was on tour in northern India. One morning Master gave me an individual sitting. I felt deeply absorbed, and lost to this world. Towards the end of the sitting, for a few minutes, I suddenly felt myself floating in an ocean of brilliance. Brilliance is perhaps not the right description. Luminescence would be more apt. All around me was nothing but sky — nothing but sky above me, below me and all around me. Perhaps I should call it space instead of sky. I was seated in the usual meditation posture, and I was floating serenely in that space which was a luminous soft blue in appearance. There was no one else, nothing else, in the whole universe but me. Not even Master! It was an ecstatic experience. Even when I became momentarily conscious during meditation the impression persisted that I was alone, absolutely and blissfully alone, in the whole immensity of space! After the sitting Master asked me how I felt. I described my experience to him. Master said, "You have been given a taste of Eternity. This generally comes at higher levels but you have been given it today."

I asked Master how this state could be made permanent, my own as it were. Master laughed and said, "*Puja* is the only method. I mean meditation, as we are taught to do it. But I tell you one thing. In *puja* the head must bend in submission. If you are conscious that you are doing *puja* then that is not *puja*. I will tell you another thing. In *puja* we go to God to receive His Grace. God has everything. After all He is God! So He has everything. But what happens when we go to Him? We go with small bags. What can He fill inside such a small bag? Therefore we must become deserving vessels for His Grace. This is essential. And this is what we do by our practice of meditation and cleaning. We are transformed into vessels fit to receive His Grace when He wishes to pour it into us.

"There is another thing I will tell you. People talk of searching for God. This is not the right attitude, in my opinion. If you search for anything that thing will be hiding from you. If search is there then that thing for which you are searching will make the distance between you longer and longer. **When I know God is there, where is the question of search?** Really speaking searching for God means searching for yourself. That is, the idea of search is cut off. What is the use of wasting your whole life in searching? We must do, not search." Master let out a great laugh and continued, "You know your son is at home, but you go and search for him in the market! I will tell you one thing. Search in your house, your heart, and you will find Him!"

On one occasion when Master was present at Madras, I had an individual sitting with sister Kasturi.

The sitting was very deep. I felt myself plunging deeper and deeper into a sort of non-conscious state. At the peak of this feeling I found myself in total darkness. There was a pinpoint of brilliance in front of me. I felt I was moving fast towards it. I looked back, and found a small aperture of light there too. By its reflection I could see I was moving fast on some sort of rails. I knew I was inside a long tunnel. I faced forwards again. I moved on rapidly, and suddenly found myself on my feet outside the tunnel, in brilliant sunlight. I found a very large crystal ball some distance away from me. I looked into it from where I was, and found the face and figure of my Master in it. As I walked towards it, and covered half the distance to it, I found the figure of my Master had changed into that of Lalaji, the Grand Master. I continued to walk towards it. As I came up to it, I found the figure had changed again. Lalaji had vanished, and what I found was my own face in it! I related this experience to Master immediately. Master was very pleased. He smiled and said, "This is a very good experience. People say lose yourself and find God, but in reality you lose yourself to find your Self. This is the truth, and I am happy you experienced it in your meditation. It is all Lalaji's Grace."

Later, the same evening, Master was alone for a brief period. He reverted to my experience and said, "Meditation is the only way. But it must be correctly done. Meditation really means that the mind may be accustomed to the Centre itself, instead of working elsewhere. At the human level the mind is wandering hither and thither, dragging us with it. It takes work from us! But by meditation we regulate it, and start taking work from it. I tell you an important thing. The mind is the instrument of realisation. It is also the instrument of our downfall. Now people talk of concentration. Concentration is the method of revelation. Meditation is the method of realisation. Concentration can reveal the nature of the object or thing concentrated upon, but it cannot lead to realisation. If you want to know the condition of an abhyasi just concentrate upon it, and the condition will come before you. Verify with the heart and it will give you the signal whether it is correct. But I am telling you a very important thing. Concentration can reveal everything but not God. If you concentrate upon God you cannot see Him because there is no thought! Only the Divine can see the Divine! Now people want to reach their goal. But the main difficulty is that people turn their backs to the sun and then search for it. Who is to blame if they find only shadows and not the Reality? If you want to move towards the sun, close your eyes and then walk towards it. Walk in faith. Now the question comes, how to walk with closed eyes. You may stumble and fall. So you need someone's help to guide you. You need a Master who can walk to the sun with his eyes open, and who can take you safely with him to your goal."

Continuing the same subject, Master said, "The Master must be a capable guide, one who has himself travelled on this road and reached the destination. Otherwise the person cannot guide us. So we have to be careful in the choice of a guide. Such a person must himself have become merged in the Ultimate. Then only he can help us. A guru is for service of others, but nowadays it is difficult to find a person who is out to serve humanity. Rather they want service themselves. I will tell you an enjoyable story. A person went to a guru and prayed to be accepted as his disciple. The guru made a lot of conditions. He said the chela must wake up early in the morning and prepare the guru's break-

fast. Then he must wash the guru's clothes, prepare
lunch and have everything ready. In the afternoon when
the guru rests he must massage his feet. It went on like
this. The person listened patiently. When the guru
finished, this person quietly said, 'please accept me as
your guru!' Is it not an enjoyable story? There is no
harm in a disciple offering personal service to the
Master, but the Master must not demand it. When the
disciple needs personal service the Master must be willing to offer it. That is real humility and surrender. One
who has surrendered to the Ultimate must feel that he
has surrendered to the whole of creation. That is the
true state of surrender. Really speaking, merging starts
from love, and surrender starts from love and dependency. Don't try for surrender, because when you try the
self is there. The real way is to be dependent. Try to
create total dependency. I am telling you one thing.
Surrender is complete only when you feel yourself surrendered to every being even if it is a fool or an animal.
A true state of surrender makes absorbency possible.
When there is absorbency in the Divine then every cell
of the body becomes energy, and then that becomes its
own absolute, that is, it becomes Divine! Master
prepares the field. The Divine does the work of trans-
forming matter into energy, and energy into its
absolute. You see the wonder of this work! It all comes
when one attracts the gaze of the Master. What do we
know of God? A direct approach to God is not possible.
A guru of calibre alone can lead the abhyasi up to God.

"God is the subtlest Being, and you must try to become as subtle as possible. The more subtle you
become the better, because by this method you come
nearer to God. So please try to become more subtle.
My problems are only so long as the abhyasi has not
crossed the *pind pradesh* (heart region). All the work is

only in this region. Also much time is taken in this region for the work. After crossing the heart region my work becomes easy. When the rings of splendour are crossed then I have nothing to do with the abhyasi. After that Nature takes up the work. Now you may ask, 'If Nature takes up the work after the rings of splendour are crossed, why cannot Nature do the work in the lower regions too?' It is a small matter. Nature can doubtless do the work but some persons are 'permitted' to do this work, that is all. Such persons are the Masters of calibre, because when permission for the work is given, the powers necessary for it is also automatically given. This is the secret of Nature that when work is given the necessary power to do the work is also given."

On one occasion Shri Ishwar Sahai spoke about realisation. His idea appealed to me very much. He said, "What is realisation? Most people don't know what this means. Some persons think that when they have a feeling of peace, of *shanti*, that is realisation. Some people think that if by their practices they get some happiness, that is realisation. But all this is not correct. Realisation means to become all that God is, and to have all that He has, that is, to become Divinised. That is what realisation really means."

I have heard several persons speaking on this subject, but wishing to know from Master himself what realisation really means, I requested him to explain this. Master said, "Realisation is such a thing that if some one discovered its secret as to what it really is, then he will not want it. I am telling you one thing. When I was an abhyasi, I one day asked my Master Lalaji Maharaj, 'Sir, you have spent a lot of time and effort on me and, from my side, I have also put in considerable effort. Is it all only for this?' Lalaji answered, 'Yes, all this has been done only for this. But you seem to think little of this condition. May I ask you a question? Suppose I were to take away this condition from you for just 5 minutes, how will you feel?' I told my Master that rather than have this happen it would be preferable for me to die! Then Lalaji answered, 'See, realisation is such a condition which we may perhaps think of as valueless, but without it our very existence is impossible.' But," added Master, "I am not prepared to reveal its secret yet. But one thing I will tell you. If realisation can be explained, it will no longer be realisation. If God can be explained or defined He ceases to be God. Both these things can't be limited. I am giving you this hint! I will tell you one more thing. When a person has attained the state of realisation then self is gone. At that stage if you try to meditate, the self will not come to your mind at all."

I was once eager to know how the liberation of a soul can be done, or is done by Master. Master laughed. He said, "Is that all? Liberation is a small thing. I tell you every sincere abhyasi of this Mission will have it. But that is only the beginning of spirituality. Liberation may give some idea of freedom for which people crave. But what is freedom? I tell you one thing. The thieves are all put into jail and locked up. The warders who guard them are also inside the jail. But one thinks himself to be a prisoner while the other thinks he is free. Do you understand the difference? Really speaking both are in prison, but one feels free! So it is in the mind, this idea of freedom. But I tell you one thing, the warden has the idea of freedom but he is really in jail! So the real freedom is when there is freedom from freedom itself."

I requested Master to explain whether death could be considered a liberation in itself. Some people feel that this is so. Master replied, "Death does not solve the problems of life, but it creates intricacies for the next life. Death sends one to another state so that one may not feel the continuity of trouble. There must be some pause in between this life and the next life to come. Men are kept in dungeons. But if they are there for years in a gloomy dungeon they will require a change. So they are brought out to exercise once in a while before they go into it again. Death is like that. Really speaking only fools die, and not the saints. Saints are everlasting in their own regime. So, death is of value for the other troubled persons. For the saints it is an un-revealed object. Now I tell you something very important. Life in life should be our real object."

At one time I had written a letter to Master about this idea of freedom, saying I did not feel free at all, and requested clarification. Master replied to me thus: "Why do you care for liberation when you yourself liberate something for the good of others? What you have asked shows that there is liberty in you but the feeling of liberty is not there. I think you want to develop a feeling of that in yourself. That is, you want to see the eye from the eye!! Care not for what is happen-ing! Await not for what is going to happen! In my opinion freedom is useless if it gives you the idea of freedom. Freedom and feeling cannot remain together. If freedom is there in its naked form the feeling will be away from it, and vice versa."

Some time after this, perhaps four or five months later, I had occasion to write to Master to put before him a peculiar condition of laziness which was develop-ing in my self. I called it laziness in my letter, but it was really a deep-seated disinclination for activity of any sort. It was blissful in a way, but I wanted Master to clarify this condition. Because it pertains to the subject of realisation, I relate this matter here. Master wrote to me in reply, "At the point of realisation a man becomes generally lazy. He likes to live in a place where activity is not there. In such a case the person should be alert that the laziness does not become predominant and his work suffers because of it. **Laziness is the life of the Soul and activity is the life of the ego.** Both should be moderate." Some time later when I personally met Master I discussed this again. Master laughed and said, "Don't worry about it. It is a very good condition for which much prayer is necessary even by sages. I will tell you one thing. I am very lazy myself but I do a lot of work in that condition! I tell you there is activity in inactivity, and that is the highest type of work. Only a *sankalp* is necessary at the beginning that such and such a thing may be done, and it is done. Even the time can be set for it, that it should be completed in so many hours or days, and it will happen exactly like that. But will must be there, a firm unfailing will. By Lalaji's Grace all this is possible."

This 'quiet' or 'rest' of the contemplative mystic has been the wonder of the world. It is apparently contradictory that a person at rest works in a way in which the most active person cannot do so. Ruysbroeck has said, "The paradoxical quiet of the contemplative is but the outward stillness essential to inward work. God is Eternal Rest! That which to us is action, to Him they declare, is rest." Evelyn Underhill says, "It remains a paradox of the mystics that the passivity at which they appear to aim is really a state of the most intense activity; more, that where it is wholly absent no great creative action can take place." One of the great mystics, Boehme, has written, "The passivity of contemplation, then, is a necessary preliminary of spiritual energy; an essential clearing of the ground. It withdraws the tide of consciousness from the shores of sense, and stops the wheel of imagination." Meister Eckhart, another great mystic, sums up the mystical view thus: "By cutting us off from the temporal plane, the lower kind of reality, contemplation gives the Eternal plane, and the powers which can communicate with that plane, their chance!"

The greatest clue to this mystery is however given by Master himself in his principle of invertendo. Simply put, anything which appears as it does at a lower level appears as its opposite in the higher manifestation. Therefore what appears as action at the normal level appears as inaction at the higher level! I believe this to be the clearest and simplest explanation of this cosmic law which Master has enunciated for us.

A great secret which Master teaches for our quick progress to our goal is that we should destroy our own small creation, which keeps us so tied down to it and to this world. "Destroy your own creation, and God comes! For everything there is a base. If you destroy this base then the Divine comes." This great secret was revealed to me when I referred to him a somewhat vivid dream I had. I dreamt that I was seated near my Master. Suddenly two eggs, or egg-like objects, fell out of my mouth and two snakes came out of them. They were long black snakes. Master said, "Don't allow them to get back inside you. This is your work. In this I can do nothing." I immediately made a strong will, transmitted, and cut the snakes into pieces and threw them away. Interpreting this Master wrote to me, "This is a very good dream, and a revealing one. One is a real egg, and its destruction indicates that the possibility of a next life for you is now destroyed. The other egg indicates your own creation, and its destruction shows that this creation of yours, too, has been destroyed. Really it is a very good dream." And then he concluded with that significant advice, "Destroy your own creation — God comes! For everything there is a base. If you destroy the base then the Divine comes!"

I have called liberation a 'gift'. It is a gift of the Master. Master once told me that the moment most appropriate, or easy, for liberation is the moment of death. He said, "At the moment of death it is very easy to liberate anybody. I just take him and put him up there." He raised his hand, pointing from a low level to a high level, as if removing a bottle from a lower shelf and putting it on a higher shelf!! "Later on it becomes difficult. The soul must not have taken rebirth. Suppose it has taken rebirth and I liberate it, the person it has been reborn as will die! You see this difficulty! And if it has taken several rebirths then nothing can be done. So I say try for it in this life itself. Who is to say whether the Master can be free to serve you at the exact moment of your death? So try for it now. I tell you one thing. **Heart is heart if it is diverted to God. Soul is soul if it jumps into the ultimate Reality.** We have to try to reach the changeless state. When we have a goal like that then changes are necessary. Changes develop power for the Ultimate growth. There are many intelligent persons, but they don't try to achieve that which is most important. Such people are not really intelligent. You know my definition of intelligence. **Intelligence is that which is inwardly tangible. I call him an intellectual who is inwardly talented — and when talent makes an inward search.** Such a man is intelligent, really speaking!"

Master's generosity is so extreme that it can be classed as nothing but Divine. The Mission is full of abhyasis who, by Master's Grace, have achieved the point of liberation, and are continuing with their further development under his Divine guidance. This we can consider a guru's service due to the abhyasi. But what about cases where Master has liberated souls on other considerations than that of abhyas under him? Such cases reveal his extreme generosity to those who have come under his protection. But having said all this, liberation yet remains a lower order of attainment within the total scope of possibilities available under the Sahaj Marg yogic system. I quote Master once again to support this view. "The goal of human life at its lowest is liberation, and this is thought to be all and enough. But the happier man is he who steps further into the realm of God. In my opinion liberation is a very narrow view of the Reality because we have to travel on and on to reach the Ultimate destination of man. When the charm of liberation is there we forget the next and real step, and that is a common error in human beings. It is also the fault of the Master if he does not encourage his disciples to go to the Highest, which we call *laya avastha* or absorption in Brahman. When a man gets into the central region and crosses the seven rings of splendour he enters into the stateless state. Then he goes further on. At this stage divine wisdon dawns followed, finally, by the vision of the Absolute. But the journey does not end here, because the turn of *laya avastha* now comes. What I have now written is the work of God. Only He can do it. Although it is the end of all our activities still there is something there. This I have referred to as 'swimming in the Infinite'. When the *laya avastha* in Brahman commences there is a very fast rotation below the navel, and there control is needed. This is the work of the Master. Then the same rotary movement travels above and reaches, by stages, the occipetal prominence. Now the progress is complete! Sometimes a little force continues in the brain, but this diminishes gradually. Now we have attained a condition which is hardly ever bestowed upon human beings. It is bestowed on him alone who is dead to the world and alive solely to God alone. In other words such a one becomes a 'living dead.' No amount of *bhakti* or *tapas* can bring about such a result. The only way is to attach ourselves to a Master who has got this stateless state, divorcing every other worship except that of God-Absolute in right form."

Liberation is a mere gift, and a cheap one at that, as Master himself asserts. When we ask for this we are merely beggars, though begging for a higher thing than material benefits. The essence of Sahaj Marg teaching is that we should seek Master for himself alone, not for what he can give us. We should ask for nothing **from** him, we should ask him to give us himself. For such an aspirant a Master longingly waits, hoping against hope that such a one will come. As Master once told me, with near grief in his voice, "It is not as difficult to find a true Master as it is to find a true disiciple. This is a very rare thing."

Several years ago, when I was at Tirupathi for the dedication of the Mission's ashram building constructed there, I heard a beautiful and moving story concerning Sister Kasturi. On one of her early visits to Tirupathi with Master, some one had offered to take her to Tirumalai and show her the famous temple to which pilgrims from all over the country flock in thousands all around the year. Sister Kasturi is reported to have smiled quietly, pointed to Master, and said, "When I am with the Creator Himself, what need is there for me to look at His creation?"

The immortal cry of that great Sufi mystic, Rabia, is very revelant here.

> "O God! Whatever share of this world
> Thou hast allotted to me,
> bestow it on Thine enemies.
> and whatever share of the next world
> Thou hast allotted to me,
> bestow it on Thy friends.
> Thou art enough for me."

> "O God! If I worship Thee in fear of Hell,
> burn me in Hell;
> and if I worship Thee in hope of Paradise,
> exclude me from Paradise;
> but if I worship Thee for Thine own sake
> withhold not Thine Everlasting Beauty!"

—Jesus

That we get God through the guru alone is the greatest single truth that Hinduism has stated again and again. The guru is God, says this profoundest of religions. We have to realise the truth of this in our lives.

I had an individual sitting with Sister Kasturi towards the end of 1972, if I remember right. The sitting started off with an obstruction in my experience. I felt that there was a road-roller blocking my path. After some time I overcame this and went on. I found a huge personality seated Buddha-like right in my way. He was golden in colour, and magnificent in appearance. His face was full of an unearthly beauty, and was tinged with the golden glow of the sun. It was Lalaji, the Grand Master. I then seemed to fall forward, and to fall right into him. The sitting ended at this stage.

I related this to Siser Kasturi. She said, "Yes, there was the initial obstruction. I saw it like a hand-cart lying across your path. Your experience of Lalaji is correct. What a wonderful way ours is! Brother, a great secret has been revealed to you today. **When one starts achieving laya with our Master, he is also automatically achieving laya with Lalaji.** This is the most important secret revealed in this experience." Later I thought over this and it flashed into my mind as a revelation that this would then mean our automatically achieving *laya* in Brahman because the Master and Grand Master have both attained *laya avastha* with Brahman. This experience was given to me by Master's Grace to prove to me, in my own conscious experience, that *laya* with the Master is nothing but *laya* with Brahman! Of God we know nothing. We know not how or where to seek Him. But the guru is one who is sent to us precisely to teach us how, through him, to find and merge with Him!

In the immortal words of St. Augustine:

> "Man **is** what he loves.
> If he loves a stone he is a stone;
> If he loves a man he is a man;
> If he loves God — I dare not say more,
> for if I said
> that he would then be God,
> ye might stone me!"

I close this work with a prayer by Blake, a great Western mystic.

> "Oh Saviour! Pour upon me
> Thy Spirit of meekness and love.
> Annihilate the selfhood in me.
> Be Thou all my Life."

May Master give us of his own Divine Wisdom, enabling us to seek **That** which alone we should seek, and find **Him** alone whom we must find.

Postscript

On the evening of Wednesday the 15th of May 1974 I was taking group *satsangh* at the Madurai centre of our Mission. About 15 minutes had elapsed in meditation. The whole group was silent. There was not a breath or whisper of sound. A stillness pervaded the gathering. It was a very calming and soothing stillness of total relaxation and absorption. At this moment I seemed to feel Master's presence by me. I heard a voice, as if it was vibrating in my heart. To call it a voice is perhaps not correct. There was no sound as we hear it with our ears. It was more a vibration inside the heart which, in some non-sensible way, I heard as sound. What Master said was this, "Many have written about the Mission. Much has also been written about the method. Now you write about the Master." It was a command which I hastened to obey. I commenced work, two days later, on Friday the 17th of May at Munnar, feeling somewhat guilty that I had tarried two days in the process. The work was completed on Friday the 23rd August. Thus, under a direct command from my Master, this book has come into your hands.

Master has taught that we can be possessive only about three things in this Universe. These are the Master, His Mission, and His Method. Therefore the title of this book is "My Master."

To me the carrying out of this work has been an absorbing pleasure and a revelation. I pray that it may be so to you too!

Madras
1st December, '74   P. Rajagopalachari